D1114448

LIFEGOALS

LIFEGOALS

Setting & Achieving Goals to Chart the Course of Your Life

by

AMY E. DEAN

Hay House, Inc.
Santa Monica, CA

LIFEGOALS
Setting and Achieving Goals to
Chart the Course of Your Life
by Amy E. Dean

Copyright © 1991 by Amy E. Dean

All rights reserved. No part of this book may be reproduced by any mechanical, photographic, or electronic process, or in the form of a phonographic recording nor may it be stored in a retrieval system, transmitted, or otherwise be copied for public or private use—other than for "fair use" as brief quotations embodied in articles and reviews—without prior written permission of the publisher.

Library of Congress Cataloging-in-Publication Data

Dean, Amy.
    LifeGoals : setting and achieving goals to chart the course of your life / by Amy E. Dean.
        p.   cm.
    ISBN 0-937611-90-5 : $12.00
    1. Goal (Psychology) 2. Conduct of life. 3. Self-realization.
    4. Success—Psychological aspects. I. Title. II. Title: Life goals.
BF503.D42   1991
158—dc20   90-80051
                                                                CIP

Library of Congress Catalog Card No. 90-80051
ISBN: 0-937611-90-5

Internal design by Teri Stewart
Typesetting by Freedmen's Typesetting Organization,
Los Angeles, CA 90004

91 92 93 94 95 96   10 9 8 7 6 5 4 3 2 1
First Printing, January 1991

Published and Distributed in the United States by

Hay House, Inc.
501 Santa Monica Boulevard
Post Office Box 2212
Santa Monica, California 90406 USA

Printed in the United States of America on Recycled Paper

This book is dedicated to Bruce Dean.

Dad, you didn't teach me how to set goals, but you always encouraged me to be the best I could be in anything I did.

Thank you for your support and the pride you have in my work.

ACKNOWLEDGMENTS

I would like to thank Priscilla Duffy for her input and encouragement while I was writing this book. Her sound advice and invaluable contributions helped to make writing this book both challenging and enjoyable.

TABLE OF CONTENTS

INTRODUCTION

 I remember returning home late one Saturday night when I was a freshman in high school, after spending all day at a speech tournament. It was my first year as a debater, and I had entered my first tournament. My father greeted me at the door. "How'd it go?" he asked.

I gave him a tired smile. "Good. The coach said I did better than any freshman debater she had ever heard. I won two out of the four matches."

My dad beamed. "Maybe you want to be a lawyer, huh? Maybe you'll be the *best* lawyer."

I smile now as I recall that memory. "Maybe you want to be . . ." is a phrase my Dad often used in connection with any particular interest I had at the time.

"I'm going to a dance tonight, Dad."

"Maybe you want to be a dancer, Amy. Maybe you'll be the best dancer ever."

"I pitched the softball game today and won."

"Maybe you want to be a semi-pro pitcher, Amy. Maybe you'll be the best pitcher ever."

"Maybe you want to be . . ."

The only problem was, my Dad never told me *how* I could get to be the best ever, in whatever endeavor I chose. Now, as I think back to those formative high school years, I can't recall anyone—parent, teacher, guidance counselor, coach, relative—who said, *in specific terms*, what I needed *to do* in order to achieve what I wanted to be and what I wanted to accomplish in my life.

No one told me about *goals*.

But perhaps that's because my father—and others from his generation—didn't set a lot of goals. My Dad graduated from high school, went to college, joined the Navy during World War II, graduated from college, then worked in the family business until he retired. From what I've discovered, most of the males from my father's generation worked at the same jobs, often until retirement.

Their goals were to work hard, make money, and support a family. Most of the females from this same generation had limited career options: nursing, teaching, or clerical work. The major goals of their lives were to meet a man, get married, and raise a family.

Haven't times changed!

Ask adults today where they're going and how they plan to get there, and chances are they don't know. We live in a microwave, throw-away, live-for-the-moment society. People change jobs frequently, often moving up corporate ladders by jumping from one position in one company to another position in another company.

Young women today are faced with a multitude of options. Not only can they choose whatever career they want, but they can also choose to marry and raise a family, marry and not raise a family, raise a family but not marry, and so on.

When I mentioned that I was writing this book to a middle-aged friend of mine, she became very excited. "Does my daughter ever need this! She doesn't know what to do with her life. She's so young. There are so many things to do. And she's so overwhelmed."

She's overwhelmed, I thought to myself, because she doesn't know how to set goals and how to achieve the goals she sets.

When you know how to set goals and achieve these goals, you're in charge of your life. With good goal-setting and effective goal-achieving, *you* determine the direction in which you'll sail.

With goals, *you* can chart the course for your life.

LIFEGOALS can help you take control of many areas in your life—self-esteem, health and fitness, relationships, communication, career/lifework, finances, life crisis, and your connection with the spiritual world—so that you can determine *where* you're going, *how* to get there, *when* you'll get there, and *what* you want to do when you arrive.

LIFEGOALS is . . . well, my Dad might hand you a copy of this book and say, "Maybe you want to set and achieve goals in your life. Maybe you want to be a great goal-setter and goal-achiever."

LIFEGOALS can help you become a great goal-setter and an even better goal-achiever!

HOW TO USE THIS BOOK

 LIFEGOALS is not a book that needs to be read from cover to cover, in the order in which the chapters are arranged. I do recommend, however, that you read Chapter One first because this initial chapter provides the framework for defining what is meant by a goal and also details the elements necessary for designing achievable goals.

After that, you can read the chapters in any order. You may prefer to skip around, focusing on those which deal with topics where you feel your current goal-setting and goal-achieving requires help. Or you may decide to explore one chapter at a time, in depth; maybe you wish to set goals in one area and "follow-through" on the results of your goal-setting before you begin work on another. Or you can just sit back and do a "quick read" on the entire book before you do any goal-setting and achieving.

But whichever way you choose to read and utilize this book, *every* chapter is designed to make your goal-setting and achieving easier through your participation in five essential chapter components.

First, even before you begin thinking about your goals, you'll be presented with a series of statements designed to help you reflect upon the topic being explored. These statements, called YOUR MOTIVATORS, help you open up the channels of inward personal assessment in the topic area.

Second, you'll be asked to think about the purpose of your goals. Why do you want to achieve goals in a particular area? This section includes YOUR MISSION CHART that you can fill in to guide you through this part of the goal-setting process.

Third, YOUR FOCUS in each chapter provides essential background information on the topic, including guidelines for healthy and positive growth.

Fourth, YOUR GOALS section provides examples of goals in the topic area and allows ample room on the pages for you to design and record your own goals.

Finally, every chapter includes a READ ON section, a suggested reading and resource list, that offers additional information on topic areas to provide you with more challenges in your goal-setting and goal-achieving.

1 □ THE BASICS OF LIFEGOALS

How to Set and Achieve Goals

LIFEGOALS *are the desired changes (goals) you wish to bring about in different areas of your personal growth in order to improve the overall quality of your life.*

What this definition means is that a LIFEGOAL doesn't focus solely on one specific portion of your life: a career goal, a weekly savings plan, or the desire to improve the quality of your relationship with an intimate partner. LIFEGOALS address different parts of your life so that you can improve the overall quality of your daily existence. Setting goals in one particular area, such as your career or lifework, may benefit that one area but can do so to the detriment of other segments of your life.

For example, you may be able to set and achieve wonderful career goals. You may receive promotion after promotion, raise after raise, and move steadily forward as you progress in your job. Yet your marriage may suffer, your health may be poor, and your self-esteem may be low. So, while you may pride yourself on being a great success in your career, focusing your goal-setting solely upon this area may negatively impact on the other aspects of your life.

As long as your goal-setting is focused on one portion of your life *for a short period of time*, there's nothing wrong with such goal-setting. However, imagine your life as a smorgasbord, filled with a wide array of appetizing foods: meats, potatoes, vegetables, fruits, breads, desserts, and drinks. Every day you can partake of this feast. Do you fill your plate only with meats? Solely with vegetables? Just desserts? Or don't you want a little bit of everything? Not only is the latter choice more nutritionally sound, but it's also more interesting than having the same thing, day after day after day.

A friend of mine, in her youth, went through a period of time when she ate yams every day. Day in, day out, she had to have her yams. I don't know when she stopped having this yam desire. In fact, I didn't even know about this yam fetish until I went to the supermarket with her. I pulled the shopping cart up to a pile of yams and said, "Have you ever tried yams? They're really good."

"Oh, God!" she screeched in horror, then calmed down and told me about the yams from her past. Then she said, "I won't eat yams anymore. I've had enough to last me a lifetime."

To me, the moral of that story is: Too much of anything for a period of time can kill your interest in it.

So, as I stated above, if you set goals solely in one area of your life—for example, your career—your interest level may start out high. But, over time, you may find that while your achievements in that one segment may be satisfying, an undercurrent of dissatisfaction may be running through the rest of your life. You may think, "I'm a business success. But I don't know my children. I'm overweight and out of shape. I can't relax. I haven't saved a dime from my salary. The only time I feel good is when I'm at the office."

LIFEGOALS can help you take the emphasis off a focus in one specific portion of your life and distribute this attention more equally to other areas that need attention: self-esteem, health and fitness, relationships, communication, careers/lifework, your personal wealth, life crises, and your relationship with spiritual meaning. *Setting and achieving goals in all areas of your life is the goal of LIFEGOALS!*

As you will see below, not everyone knows how to set goals, even in one area of their lives. I've talked with a number of people about their experiences with goal-setting. Here are some of their responses. Do you relate to any of these thoughts, beliefs, or actions?

- *"I tend to bite off more than I can chew when I set goals."*
- *"Setting goals is like making a commitment. So I avoid setting them."*
- *"I'm reluctant to set goals because I'm afraid I'll fail."*
- *"I achieve only some of the goals I set. Setting goals is very frustrating."*
- *"I set goals but don't keep up with them."*
- *"I can't think about the future; I live day to day."*
- *"I don't know what goals I ought to have."*
- *"I never really learned how to set goals."*
- *"Every time I set a goal it seems I never reach it."*
- *"I expect complete results from my goals."*

People who don't set goals or who fail to achieve the goals they set usually fall into one, or both, of these categories:

1. They are fearful of taking risks.

They may be too afraid of the consequences of failing to meet their goals, consequences that include feelings of disappointment, depression, hopelessness, poor self-image, being stuck in the same rut, and so on. Or they may be afraid of achieving their goals because of the perceived pressure to attain other goals, to strive for perfection, to have to make changes or plan for the future, or the possibility of being perceived by others as selfish, and so on.

2. They lack the information necessary to set goals.

They may not know the basic components of goal-setting, so they may set goals that are inappropriate, unrealistic, not specific enough, or those that are too complicated. Or, perhaps they set goals that are based on satisfying the needs of others, that aren't challenging enough, or goals that can't be achieved in small steps. They may also think that their goals ought to result in "instant achievement," and therefore may abandon legitimate, effective ones because they don't realize that achieving them requires time, patience, and attention to incremental progress—not a focus on the end result.

Let's explore these two categories in greater detail.

TAKING RISKS

Before you set a goal, you must be willing to take a risk. *A goal is the end result that will help bring about a desired change, once that goal is achieved.*

Since "a desired change" is the ultimate aim of a goal, you must be willing to make that change. And making a change involves taking a risk.

Risk-taking means leaping empty-handed into a void, with the intent of creating a firm foundation. Sometimes you may take this leap and come out of it unscathed—you may ask your boss for a raise and get it. Or you may feel hurt, pain, or frustration as a result of this leap—you may ask your boss for a raise and be subjected to a litany on how poor your job performance is. But whatever the outcome, it's important to take the risk. As opera singer Beverly Sills once said, *"You may be disappointed if you fail, but you are doomed if you don't try."*

A risk, by definition, has two parts. First, it's the measure of the probability of failure. The greater the danger of failure, the greater the risk. Such a risk could be going back to school to complete a college degree after dropping out twice in the past. The probability of failure in this case, based on one's track record, is high.

Second, it's a combination of fear and the possibility of satisfaction or enthusiasm. Parachuting out of an airplane or asking someone out on a date are examples of this type of risk. While fear may be felt in both cases, success can produce exhilaration or pleasure.

But most people are not risk-takers. Negative statements that inhibit risk-taking include:

- *"It won't work; it never does."*
- *"I don't think I need to suffer in order to change; I've suffered enough already in my life."*
- *"I'm so inadequate that I'll never be able to change."*
- *"It's hopeless; nothing ever changes for the better."*

In order to begin taking risks, you need to recognize that you create your own attitudes. *Attitudes are our concious texts for choosing.* So if you have the attitude that you'll never be able to change, most likely you will not make any changes.

Likewise, your attitudes influence your experiences in life. You're accountable for your experiences because you cause them, either directly by your actions or indirectly by your choices. Because your choices shape your experiences, you can change your life by making new choices.

Think about this . . .

Changing your attitude can simply be a matter of changing the vocabulary you use:

- Change *"but"* to *"and"*
  "I really want to change, but . . ." becomes *"I really want to change, and . . ."*
- Change *"I know"* to *"I imagine"*
  "I know it's not possible," becomes *"I imagine it's not possible."*
- Change *"I can't"* to *"I prefer not to"*

"I can't give up smoking," becomes *"I prefer not to give up smoking."*

- Change *"I have to"* to *"I choose to"*
"I have to get better", becomes *"I choose to get better."*

- Change *"I should"* to *"I could"*
"I should lose weight," becomes *"I could lose weight."*

- Change *"I don't know"* to *"I can find out"*
"I don't know what to do," becomes *"I can find out what to do."*

- Change *"always"* to *"sometimes"*
"I always screw up" becomes *"I sometimes screw up."*

- Change *"never"* to *"might not"*
"My life will never get better" becomes *"My life might not get better."*

Making new choices means taking risks, and the biggest roadblock to risk-taking is fear. But by working through your fears, you can open up doors that lock you out from experiencing great potential.

There are methods I use that help me work through my fears and put me in control of it so I become a "fear manager" instead of a "fear slave."

One method, which author Susan Jeffers adhers to, is to "feel the fear, but do it anyway." When an intimate relationship I was involved in ended a couple of years ago, I was scared to stay home alone at night. But I told myself, *"It's okay to be afraid. It's a legitimate fear. Feel it. Then take a hot bath, put on your favorite pajamas, read a good book, and sleep with the lights on if you want to. Feel the fear, and you'll get through it."* And I did!

Another method that's helpful in working through fears involves gradually altering your level of comfort until you're more at ease with situations that cause you distress. Your level of comfort is determined by how much fear you can handle or deal with at one time. This comfort level varies from person to person. For example, I'm very comfortable speaking in front of large groups of people; others don't necessarily share this same level of comfort in similar situations.

On an individual basis, the level of comfort can change depending on the circumstances in an individual's life at a particular moment. When I'm tired and hungry, for example, I'm more susceptible to feeling anxious or scared.

To gradually alter your level of comfort in risk-taking, take small risks and achieve them first, rather than try to tackle a big, fear-producing risk right away. Taking the smaller risks helps you build your confidence and allows you to gradually become more comfortable with your fears. For example, to work through fears associated with a big risk such as skydiving, you could watch a skydiving film or talk to people about their own experiences with this pursuit.

Another method for working through fears involves thinking about and writing responses to the question: *What's the worst possible thing that could happen if I take this risk?*

List one or more of these "worst possible things" on the left side of a piece of paper. Then, on the right side of the paper, list actions or thoughts that can help you allevi-ate each of these fears. In this way, you can *anticipate* the fears *before* they actually happen. This practice of provid-ing methods to alleviate your fears can help you use crea-tive problem-solving to work through them.

Here's an example of the fear alleviation method:

RISK: Taking a vacation to a tropical location

Fears:	*Alleviating the Fears:*
Too much time away from work	Take some work with you.
Flying	Practice relaxation tech-niques prior to the flight; listen to a meditation tape during the flight
Lack of Money	Work out expenses be-fore hand; design a daily budget to set spending limits.
Getting sunburned	Take sunblock; work in-doors during strongest sun hours.
Being far away from home (comfort level)	Bring something from home with you (a pillow or stuffed animal)

Another roadblock to risk-taking is the tension the act may create in you and/or in the parties involved in the risk. For example, asking your boss for a raise could make your boss upset, sabotage your vacation time, alienate your coworkers, etc. Tensions, like fears, can "talk" you out of taking risks.

I work through tensions by creating an obstacle/solution chart, similar to my fear alleviation chart. I list all the obstacles (tensions) that might prevent me from taking the risk. Next, I list possible solutions to these obstacles. Then I choose what I believe to be the best solution and try it. Here's an example of this type of risk-taking chart on the right.

RISK: Talking to my intimate partner about the time he spends away from me

Obstacles	Solutions
My partner might not listen.	Discuss a different, less threatening topic first.
I might not be clear.	Write down what I want to say first.
I might start an argument.	Be prepared to end the discussion if necessary.
I might be rejected.	Talk to a friend first.

Choose a Solution: Write down what I want to say first.

Evaluate It (Tell What Happened as a Result): Because I had written down that I was sensitive to being left alone as a result of the abandonment issues from my childhood, we were able to discuss this issue with tenderness and sensitivity. I had recorded how I felt when my partner would decide to go out on his own for an evening without consulting me, and I shared these feelings. As a result, we decided to plan our times apart for the week ahead on Sunday night. It was great to be as clear as I was about this issue and to be able to reach a mutually agreeable solution without arguing.

Being ready to take a risk doesn't mean that you won't feel any fear or any tension. Fear and tension are natural reactions to taking risks. Feel them, confront them, work through them—then take your risk anyway!

Think about this . . .

The worst risk-takers are people who say, *"What do I have to lose?"* They have the attitude that if they don't succeed, such failure will validate the negative feelings they may already have about themselves.

The best risk-takers are the people who say, *"This is what I have to lose, and this is how I'll try to avoid losing it, yet I'll take the risk anyway."* While they know they may not succeed, they're willing to take the risk anyway.

As Aristotle once noted, *"What we have to learn to do, we learn by doing."*

SETTING GOALS

Remember the definition of a goal: *It's the end result that will help bring about a desired change, once the goal is achieved.* The key phrase in this definition is "end result." Any goal begins with a MISSION, or a purpose or reason for wanting to achieve the end result (the goal). Usually this mission is based on a need, want, or desire; for example: "I want to develop new friendships," "I need to quit smoking," or "I desire a better-paying job."

But these are not goals in themselves. And this is why many people do not know how to set goals. They often begin with a mission and think that's the goal.

"I want to quit smoking" is not a goal. Rather, it's the desire, need, or want of an individual—the end result of the goal. "I want to quit smoking on New Year's Day" is not a goal, even though it's more specific, because this statement continues to express a desire, need, or want.

When I set my own goal to stop smoking, I achieved it. I stopped smoking for good. Completely. Without one slip. And that's because I set a goal that included all the elements necessary to make the goal work.

A goal requires eight key elements:

1. The Mission

This provides the motivation for wanting to make the goal. For example, "I want to quit smoking."

2. The Emotional Core

The emotional core is what *you* need or want from the goal, based on your mission. For example, *"I want my clothes to smell fresh and clean. I want my breath to smell nice; I want to be able to taste my food, and I don't want to be out of breath when I reach the top of a flight of stairs."*

3. Role Model

This is the person you'd like to become or the life you'd like to have once you achieve your goal. You might choose someone whom you admire, select a picture out of a magazine (many people who set goals for losing weight do this, then tape the picture of a thinner person on their refrigerator doors), or simply visualize what changes can occur in yourself or in your life once you achieve your goal.

When I was teaching a class on goal-setting, I asked my students who or what their role models were for the goals they wished to achieve. Answers included "a thinner me," "a better golfer," "a more outgoing person," and so on. I continued going around the room. "Meryl Streep," came the next response, accompanied by the laughter of her classmates.

"Why did you select her?" I asked.

"She's rich," was the reply.

"What's your goal?" I asked her.

"To ask for a raise of fifty dollars a week this Friday."

"Then you've chosen a good role model," I told her. "If you keep the image of Meryl Streep in mind—someone who's talented, who's worth the money she makes, who's in demand, who's confident—then you're creating a very powerful role model that can help you achieve your goal."

Using a role model can help you create an enticing, promising vision that can keep you motivated as you work towards achieving your goal.

4. Commitment

Simply stated, in order to achieve your goals, you must want to achieve them. Your goals ought to be based on personal satisfaction and interests, not on what you think you ought to be doing and not on what others need, want, or expect from you. In addition, it's not a good idea to set goals designed to please others or to gain approval or love. After all, how can you be committed to someone else's goal? *Set goals for yourself because those are the goals you'll want to achieve.*

To assess your level of commitment to a goal, ask yourself two important questions:

1. *How badly do I want to achieve my goal?*
2. *Am I willing to work for it?*

If you don't want your goal badly enough, then chances are you won't be committed to the goal or to the attainment of the end result.

My parents tried to get me to stop smoking for years. My mother mailed me newspaper articles that discussed the hazards of smoking. My father reminded me about my aunt, a heavy smoker, who had died from bone cancer. But I wanted to keep smoking. And, for as long as I felt that way, nothing they said or did would make me set a goal to stop smoking. I wasn't committed to *their* goal.

When I decided to stop smoking, I didn't say, "I'll smoke the rest of this pack" or "I'll stop at midnight tonight" or "I'll wait until after the weekend." I made no bargains with myself. I was committed from the start. That level of determination kept me focused on achieving my goal, despite the physical craving I often had to start smoking again.

5. Specific Guidelines

A goal is your blueprint to progress. Because of this, the blueprint needs to be stated in specific terms, with concrete guidelines. These guidelines help you specify the plan you'll put into action to attain the goal.

For example, if your goal is to lose weight, then how much weight do you want to lose? When do you want to lose it by? How do you intend to lose it? *Be specific.*

Specific guidelines helped me stay away from smoking. I knew cigarettes and coffee went hand-in-hand, so in the mornings I drank a different hot beverage, such as herb tea, that didn't tempt me to smoke. I cut up fresh vegetables, bought sugarless mints and gum, and loaded them into my briefcase so I could take them with me to work. I combined an exercise goal—running—with my stop-smoking goal. With these specific guidelines, I was more prepared and committed to working towards my goal—and to achieving it.

Thus, *definite goals achieve definite results.*

Think about this . . .

> *"Our main business is not to see what lies dimly at a distance but to do what lies clearly at hand."*
> —Thomas Carlyle

6. Focus

Focus is the process of bringing together the resources necessary to accomplish a goal. For example, if you want to take a Europena skiing vacation, sending for travel brochures from ski resorts or talking with a travel agent can provide the focus to help you achieve the goal.

For my stop-smoking/exercise goal, I purchased books on running so I could set a reasonable goal as a beginning runner. I also priced running shoes and mapped out running routes near my home.

7. Timetable

Goals need to be placed on a timetable. Ask: How long will it take to achieve my goal? The time period you determine needs to be realistic, flexible, and, if beneficial, incremental.

A realistic timetable is based first on how long it will *realistically* (and logically) take to achieve your goal. I know one woman who wanted to lose 60 pounds by the time her friend's wedding arrived, which was two months away. Rather than focusing on how long it would actually take her to lose all 60 pounds, she stuck with her original, unrealistic timetable. Needless to say, she didn't achieve her goal.

But she could have said, "I'm going to lose two pounds a week for the next eight weeks, until my friend's wedding. Then I'll be sixteen pounds lighter. After the wedding, I'll set a new goal."

It's also important that your timetable be flexible. Even the best made plans sometimes don't work out or need to be changed because of unforeseeable circumstances.

For example, what if the woman who set a goal of asking her boss for a $50-a-week raise by Friday finds that her boss isn't in the office Friday? When this *really* happened, the woman was ready to give up her goal. "I was pysched to talk to her on Friday," she explained to me. "When she didn't show up, well, I felt I couldn't go through with my goal at another time."

Goals, and their timetables, are not cast in stone. They do not carry the force of the law. Once made, they can be revised, changed, amended, reevaluated, or expanded. Imagine the football coach who has great plans for using his star quarterback in an upcoming game. But then, three hours before the game, his quarterback sprains his wrist and can't play. Does the coach call the other team and say, "Gee, I guess we'll have to forfeit. I had a certain game plan, and now I can't follow it. It's your win."

When I related this story to the woman who wanted to scrap her plans to talk to her boss, her response was, "Yeah, but . . ."

"Yeah, but what?" I asked.

"But I said I'd do it on Friday."

"So?"

"So she didn't show up."

"So? Do you still want a raise?"

"Yes."

"Do you still feel you deserve a raise?"

"Yes."

"Then let's imagine Friday never existed. Let's imagine Monday is Friday. Can you ask her?"

"Well . . ."

"Do it! And if she isn't in on Monday, ask her Tuesday. Or ask her Wednesday. Just because your timetable didn't account for this little glitch doesn't mean you throw your goal away. Sometimes a goal depends upon the presence of someone else to achieve it. So it needs to be a little more flexible, to account for that person's schedule."

When you set a timetable for your goal, build in time for crises or setbacks that could affect your schedule. Or, set a shorter initial time period, and evaluate the progress of your goal at the end of that period before you set a new timetable.

Finally, a timetable that's broken down into smaller chunks of time can be much easier to achieve. For example, if the woman who wants to shed 60 pounds sets weekly goals of losing two pounds, then her overall goal may feel much more accessible.

For goals that need to be achieved by a specific date or within a limited time frame, an incremental timetable isn't necessary. But the saying: "A journey of a thousand miles begins with just one step," can be applied to goals that need to be achieved within a longer time period.

To help you decide which timetable will work best with the goals you set, you can classify your goals into types.

Immediate Goal

This is a goal you wish to achieve right now, within the next few minutes to the next few hours. An immediate goal could be: "I'm going to mail those letters right now" or "I'll start the laundry right after dinner."

Immediate goals, while not highly challenging, are superb motivators because they require instantaneous action in order to achieve them. People who tend to have difficulty setting goals or those who find themselves procrastinating can benefit from making those types of goals.

Organized people usually are good at setting immediate goals; they're list-makers who structure their days around crossing items off lists. These people may not real-ize they're actually setting and achieving immediate goal after immediate goal.

The only drawback to immediate goals occurs if you choose to focus *solely* on setting and achieving these goals. While immediate goals can be highly gratifying, they're not considered "investments" in the future. Also, often they do not provide a great deal of personal challenge or a high degree of risk.

Short-Term Goal

The time period for a short-term goal is from one week to one month. A short-term goal could be: "I'm go-ing to lose two pounds this week" or "I'm going to change my eating habits this month by cutting out desserts and between-meal snacking."

Short-term goals work best when weekly evaluations are included to review your progress and, if necessary, to revise your goals.

Mid-Term Goal

A mid-term goal covers the time period from one month to a year. Examples of mid-term goals include tak-ing an educational course, working on a health and fitness program, doing individual or couples therapy work, and so on.

Mid-term goals are more ambitious than immediate and short-term goals and are usually a bit more difficult to achieve. As a result, monthly review periods are often helpful in evaluating your progress.

Long-Term Goal

A two to four-year period is the time frame for a long-term goal. Usually long-term goals are focused on training or education, saving for a home, paying off a car loan, and so on.

Long-term goals require patience in order to achieve them because the results, or benefits, aren't immediate. Sometimes breaking a long-term goal down into mid-term or short-term goals helps stimulate a high level of interest throughout the time period necessary to achieve your goal.

Long-term goals involve a high degree of risk. As such, the risk carries with it the possibility of success as well as the possibility of disappointment or failure. As a result, the outcome of a long-term goal is not always assured. For example, you might invest two years studying for an M.B.A. degree and one year in a corporation after you've received your degree, only to find that you're not happy with your new career.

But long-term goals can also bring about positive changes both in the individual as well as in his or her lifestyle. Someone who invests in the training or education necessary for a career change and finds happiness on the new career path may also find improvements in personal relationships, greater financial security, a higher level of self-esteem, and so on.

Target Goal

Target goals are concerned with *lifestyle desires* (to be married or single, to have children or not have children, to live in the city or in the country, etc.), *dreams* (of living in a house by the ocean or owning a fancy sports car, for instance), and *fantasies* (of a romantic vacation in an exotic location or perhaps falling in love with a tall, dark stranger).

Due to these concerns, target goals have no timetable. Rather, target goals are often used to set shorter-term goals that have more specific time frames. However, identifying dreams, fantasies, or lifestyle choices can make it easier to determine the methods that can be used to achieve your target goals.

Some goals require an open-ended time frame, such as my stop-smoking goal, which has no real "end," or a goal that involves personal growth, healing, or recovery. But with such goals, it's still important to set specific time periods for reassessment, praise, or evaluation while working on the goal.

8. Assessment/Achievement

The final component of goal setting is determining a time when the goal and/or your progress towards the goal can be assessed. This assessment time allows you to evaluate whether the goal is still valid, because time and circumstances can change your original goal. This time also allows you to revise your goal, if necessary, and to recognize and celebrate achievement of your goal.

I decided to evaluate my progress in my stop-smoking goal every two weeks. This gave me time to "check-in" and see how I was doing and how I was feeling. I weighed myself to make sure I wasn't gaining weight. I reviewed my exercise program and made changes, such as mapping out different running routes. And, at the end of every two-week period, I bought myself a present to congratulate myself on my progress.

Think about this . . .

When you make a goal, you're building a bridge between who you are now and who you want to be in the future. But, as Winston Churchill once advised, *"It is a mistake to look too far ahead. Only one link in the chain of destiny can be handled at a time."* Be prepared to build "new" bridges (to make new goals) or repair "old" bridges (to assess and revise current goals) when necessary.

In the beginning of this chapter I mentioned that LIFEGOALS are the goals you set in many different areas of your life. This book explores eight specific areas. To effectively focus on each of these areas in your goal-setting—which is the aim of LIFEGOALS—I recommend that you create and try to achieve *at least one goal* in each of the eight areas after you have read the chapters individually or have completed the book.

Your goals don't have to be ambitious, target goals; they can be simple, immediate goals. You can set one goal in one area at a time and focus on achieving that goal before moving on to the next area. You can set two or more related or unrelated goals in different areas and try to achieve them simultaneously. For example, related goals could include working towards greater intimacy in your relationship with your partner while you use active listening in your communication. Unrelated goals could include quitting smoking while you set aside 20 minutes a day to meditate while you also enroll in a course to help your job advancement.

Or you can alternate working on goals in different areas, maybe working one week on a finance-related goal and then spending the next month focused on a relationship-related goal.

Setting goals in each area will help you look at the various parts of your life, evaluate changes you'd like to make, and see the vision of what you and your life could become.

LIFEGOALS PREPLANNING

Before you begin goal-setting, take a moment to think about the parts of your life that could really benefit from this task. Listed below are eight major topics discussed in this book. Reflect upon each area by asking yourself:

- *"Have I already set goals in this area?"*
- *"If so, am I happy with the outcome of these goals?"*
- *"In what ways could I benefit from setting goals (or making new goals) in this area?"*
- *"If I could see myself as I'd really like to be in this area, what would I look like? What would my life be like?"*

Then use your responses to help you formulate goals in each area as you work through the book.

- *SELF-ESTEEM:* How You Feel About Yourself
- *HEALTH AND FITNESS:* How You Treat Yourself

- *RELATIONSHIPS:* How You Interact With Others
- *COMMUNICATION:* How You Verbalize Who You Are and What You Want
- *CAREER/LIFEWORK:* How to Achieve Challenge, Satisfaction, and Fulfillment From Your Career or Lifework
- *YOUR PERSONAL WEALTH:* How to Manage Your Money to Enrich Your Life
- *LIFE CRISIS:* How to Overcome Personal Crisis Through the Process of Healing and Recovery
- *YOUR SPIRITUAL SELF:* How You Connect Your Physical and Emotional Nature with a Spiritual Understanding

READ ON

Changing Your Life, by Strephon Kaplan-Williams, MFCC, Journey Press, Berkeley, CA, 1984, 1985, 1987.

Feel the Fear and Do It Anyway, by Susan Jeffers, Ph. D., Fawcett Columbine, 1987.

How People Change, by Allen Wheelis, Harper & Row, 1973.

If You Don't Know Where You're Going, You'll Probably End Up Somewhere Else, by David Campbell, Ph.D., Argus Communications, Allen, TX, 1974.

The Path of Least Resistance, by Robert Fritz, Fawcett Columbine, 1984.

Wishcraft: How to Get What You Really *Want,* by Barbara Sher, Ballantine, 1979.

2 □ SELF-ESTEEM

How You Feel About Yourself

 Self-esteem is defined as *the emotional, physical, and spiritual value you place upon yourself.* In the broadest sense, self-esteem is composed of two elements: *self-competence,* or the ability to confront the challenges life presents and to design constructive solutions to everyday problems; and a feeling of *genuine worth,* or the right to recognize, respect, and pursue your interests and needs.

To have *high self-esteem* is to feel competent and worthy in coping with the challenges in life and in being happy.

To have *low self-esteem* is to feel inappropriate to life or wrong; wrong not necessarily about one issue or another, but wrong as a person.

To have *average self-esteem* is to fluctuate between feeling appropriate and inappropriate (right and wrong as a person), to manifest these inconsistencies by sometimes choosing wisely and sometimes not so wisely, and, on the whole, achieving a balance somewhere between high self-esteem and low self-esteem.

People who have *healthy self-esteem* are not "at war"

(in conflict) with themselves or with others. People with average or high self-esteem often experience healthy self-esteem.

YOUR MOTIVATORS

Each of the following statements reflects some of the thoughts, feelings, and behaviors of a person who has a healthy level of self-esteem. Do these statements accurately reflect your current level of self-esteem?

- *"I believe in myself."*
- *"I'm a worthwhile human being."*
- *"I'm attractive."*
- *"I like myself."*
- *"I do things for myself as well as for others."*
- *"My needs are important."*
- *"I accept my feelings."*
- *"I share my feelings openly and honestly."*
- *"My growth is important."*
- *"I like to make changes."*
- *"I'm confident."*
- *"I take care of myself when I'm sick."*
- *"I'm patient with myself."*
- *"I forgive myself when I make a mistake."*
- *"I let go of anger easily."*
- *"I know what I want for myself."*

- *"I can do whatever I set out to do."*

- *"I'm not perfect, and that's just fine."*

- *"What matters is what I think of myself, not what others think of me."*

- *"I deserve good things."*

- *"I accomplish good things in my life."*

- *"I can make decisions that are right for me."*

- *"I have many good qualities."*

People with a healthy level of self-esteem are often comfortable with themselves. They may not always like their body image or the way they behave, but they can accept who they are, how they look, and how they act.

Although they enjoy the compliments and attention shown to them by others, they don't depend upon such approval to help them feel better about themselves. Judgments and criticisms may hurt them, but they try not to let the negative statements of others, no matter how close these people are to them, influence or change how they feel about themselves. But that's not always easy to do! In my work with adult children—those who grew up in dysfunctional childhood homes—I interact with people who struggle every day to rise above the unfair and sometimes cruel judgments and criticisms thrown in their direction by unhealthy parents, spouses, and even children.

When we discuss how to develop self-esteem, these people will often tell me how difficult it is to hear negative statements such as *"You're stupid"* or *"You'll never amount to anything"* and to not react by trying to change themselves, their actions, or their behaviors in order to please others and gain their approval.

"It's not easy accepting who you are and feeling good about yourself when there are those around you who will shoot you down," I agree with them. "But think about this. Write down the names of three people whose opinions you truly respect and value on one side of a sheet of paper. Now write down three judgments or criticisms that you've been told by others in your life on the other side of the paper. Look at the two lists and ask yourself: *Would any of the three people you listed ever say any of the three statements to you?*"

When judgments or criticisms land in your lap, consider the source. Then think about how much respect you have for this person's opinion. Finally, keep in mind Marshall Shelley's outlook on criticism, from his book, *Well-Intentioned Dragons*.

> *"Solitary shots should be ignored, but when they come from **several directions** (author's emphasis), it's time to pay attention. As someone once said, 'If one calls you a donkey, ignore him. If two call you a donkey, check for hoof prints. If three call you a donkey, get a saddle.'"*

Like everyone else, people with a healthy level of self-esteem have good days and bad days. But they don't let outside influences dictate how they feel about themselves. People with a healthy level of self-esteem usually don't "beat themselves up" when things go wrong. They're resilient to life's ups and downs and are less likely to succumb to feelings of defeat or despair. They make decisions and take risks. They're motivated and energetic. They're not afraid to experience joy and happiness.

People with a healthy level of self-esteem enjoy life and enjoy themselves.

If feeling good about yourself feels so good, then why doesn't everyone have a healthy sense of self-esteem?

I think part of the answer lies in the messages that people are given when they're growing up. For instance, if you're told that you're no good, that you're unattractive, or that you'll never measure up to your brother or sister or father or mother, then you'll most likely grow into adulthood with a low sense of self-esteem. You'll probably feel that nothing you do will ever be good enough.

I think another part of the answer lies in how well four basic emotional needs are satisfied in childhood. Everyone has these four needs. They're integral components in an individual's psychological development.

1. The Need to Be Noticed

This means someone notices you and recognizes that you have thoughts and feelings.

2. The Need for Acceptance

This means someone enjoys your company and likes to be around you.

3. The Need for Independence

This means you're capable of making some of your decisions, even if these decisions are not always "right."

4. The Need to be Loved

This means you receive reassurance from someone that you're loved.

How well each of these needs is satisfied in your childhood has a great impact on how you may feel about yourself not only as a growing child, but also later on in life as a maturing adult.

If you didn't have these needs met or satisfied in your childhood, chances are you'll spend most of your adult life struggling to get these needs met. So rather than focus on yourself and your personal growth, you may try to get others to focus on you and help you meet these needs.

I can illustrate this with a story from my own life. As a baby, I was adopted into a home where I had an alcoholic mother. Because she couldn't take care of me, I was taken from this home and placed in a foster home until my adoptive parents divorced. My father remarried when I was seven years old; by that time, I had already had three mothers—my birth mother, my alcoholic adoptive mother, and my foster "mother."

When my fourth mother, my father's second wife, came into my life, I often visited my friends' homes and asked their mothers if they would be my mother. I became very attached to schoolteachers and camp counselors. Later on in life, I searched for my birth mother and my alcoholic mother. I now know why I did these things—I tried to get others to satisfy needs that weren't met in my childhood.

I think a final reason why people have low self-esteem relates to how well they cope with the difficulties that face them in adulthood. Some people, unfortunately, face terrific burdens and hardships in adult life. Tragedies come in many forms and can have a great impact. The higher someone's level of self-esteem is *prior* to such difficulties, the easier it can often be for that person to work through an understanding and acceptance and to deal with the loss or pain. But sometimes people find it difficult to carry on. They may lose sight of their own personal growth and recovery for such a long period of time that they no longer care about themselves or feel good about their lives. So their self-esteem suffers.

But the reasons for low self-esteem aren't as important as how low self-esteem affects individual growth in adulthood. It can be difficult for people with a low sense of self-esteem to raise their level of self-esteem—to feel better about themselves—when they're influenced by beliefs such as the following. Do you share in any of these beliefs?

- *"I need to be affirmed by others."*
- *"I always think I could be better than I am."*
- *"I don't feel I'm good in any one area."*
- *"I'm very sensitive to criticism."*
- *"I know my work is good, but I often question its quality."*
- *"I have a hard time believing I'm important."*

- *"No matter what I do, it's never enough."*
- *"Everyone else is always better than I am."*
- *"I don't give myself credit for the things I do."*
- *"I'm afraid to look at myself."*
- *"Feeling good is temporary."*
- *"I try to be too perfect."*

Such beliefs, or attitudes, can sabotage personal growth, stifle creativity, and snuff out motivation for making positive changes. No matter where these statements originated—from a dysfunctional childhood, from personal failure, from a lack of confidence, or for whatever reason—their impact can *destroy* self-esteem. And until efforts are made to change them, they will function as self-defeating beliefs—attitudes that prevent an individual from living up to his or her true potential.

Notice I wrote these attitudes need to be *changed,* not *eliminated.* It's a common myth, believed by those who have a low or average level of self-esteem, that people who have high self-esteem *never* feel depressed or discouraged or negative. Another myth is that someone with a healthy level of self-esteem *never* has a self-defeating attitude. Such myths are simply that. People with healthy self-esteem can feel as insecure, doubtful, hopeless, and so on as the next person.

But the edge that their healthy self-esteem gives them is the confidence to work through such feelings and get to the other side—a side with a positive outlook that results in positive growth.

LIFEGOALS can help you raise your level of self-esteem by helping you eliminate self-defeating beliefs from your life and by providing you with self-esteem-building tools that can help you strengthen your feelings of competence and worth. But SELF-ESTEEM LIFE-GOALS will not take away your faults, prevent you from having negative feelings, or make you feel superior or better than others. Rather, SELF-ESTEEM LIFEGOALS will help you feel more comfortable with yourself and more competent as a human being.

SELF-ESTEEM LIFEGOALS can help you work through such common dilemmas such as:

- *"Why can't I treat myself as well as I treat others?"*
- *"How can I let go of the need for the approval of others?"*
- *"Why can't I see the good qualities others say I have?"*
- *"Is focusing on myself selfish?"*
- *"Will working on self-esteem make me less afraid of myself?"*
- *"Why can't I do the things I want to do?"*

When you make SELF-ESTEEM LIFEGOALS, you're giving yourself the opportunity to improve *the quality of your relationship with yourself.* This can change your entire outlook on life from one that's negative to one that's positive.

Think about this . . .

No matter who you are, it's tempting to look at others and wonder, "Why can't I be as good as they are?"

In an interview in *Esquire* magazine, this is what Robert Redford had to say about his best friend, Paul Newman: *"I'm driving home and thinking to myself: . . . here's old Paul. What is he? Sixty? Sixty-one? I don't know. He looks great, feels great, has alot of money, gives to great causes, loves his wife, he races his cars when he wants to, makes a movie when he wants to, he's incredibly happy and still has that face that looks the way it did when he was twenty. God, by the time I got home, I wanted to shoot myself."*

YOUR MISSION

To begin setting SELF-ESTEEM LIFEGOALS, first determine a few missions for your goals and outline them on the SELF-ESTEEM MISSIONS CHART. Your missions are based on:

1. Your particular self-esteem problem areas (Who Are You Now?);

2. What you need or want from your goals (What Do You Want to Achieve?); and

3. The type of person you'd like to become or the life you'd like to have once you achieve your goals (Who Will You Be? or How Will You Be?)

SELF-ESTEEM MISSIONS CHART

Who Are You Now?
Example: *I'm a person who is too hard on myself when I don't do everything perfectly.*

1. _____

_____

2. _____

_____

What Do You Want to Achieve?
Example: *I want to relax when I make a mistake.*

1. _____

_____

2. _____

_____

Who Will You Be? or How Will You Be?
Example: *I see a person who is smiling and relaxed, easy to be with, and mellow.*

1. _____

_____

2. _____

_____

Your Mission
Example: *I want to create a goal that will help me stop being such a perfectionist and will allow me to forgive myself if and when I make a mistake.*

1. _____

_____

2. _____

_____

YOUR FOCUS

All About Self-Esteem

In the beginning of this chapter I mentioned the two elements that help to define self-esteem in the broadest sense—self-competence and genuine worth. But how do you develop each of these qualities so you can achieve a healthy level of self-esteem?

I believe self-esteem is made up of ten integral parts, which play important roles in contributing to self-competence and personal worth. To develop your self-esteem, it's important not only to understand the contribution each part makes to an overall sense of self, but also to strengthen the impact each has upon self-esteem. This strengthening process can involve setting goals to change unhealthy patterns of behavior or negative attitudes to healthier behaviors and a more positive outlook.

The more committed you feel about your personal development in each of these ten areas, the healthier your self-esteem will be and the more confidence you can have in everything you do.

1. Self-Acceptance

This is what self-esteem is all about. Self-acceptance means that you can accept what you feel, who you are, what you look like, and how you act at any given moment. Developing self-acceptance begins with eliminating statements about yourself that begin with ''I wish . . ."; for example, "I wish I had curly hair," "I wish I was smarter," "I wish I was thinner," etc.

Even though you may wish there were things about yourself that you could change—a scar or a blemish on your body, a wider love handle than you'd like to have, or controlling behaviors with other people—these things are all part of you. Self-acceptance means not turning away from parts of you, whether they are good, bad, or ugly, because to do so means that you're turning away from yourself.

When you have a high level of self-acceptance, you don't reject these things about yourself. You accept them by acknowledging that they're part of you; they help define who you are at this very moment. Such acceptance doesn't mean you can't or won't change these things; it simply means that whether or not you change, you still accept yourself for who you are.

The goal for developing self-acceptance is to see who you are and to accept yourself completely and unreservedly. When you do, you can believe:

- *"I'm okay."*
- *"I like my appearance."*
- *"I appreciate myself for who I am."*
- *"I feel happy with the things I do and the way I do them."*

Think about this . . .

Ralph Waldo Emerson once said that individuality is *". . . being one's self and reporting accurately what we see and are."*

An exercise to help you develop self-acceptance involves such a process of self-assessment and self-honesty. It's called *"I Look in the Mirror, and What Do I See?"*

Stand in front of a full-length mirror, with or without clothing, and look at your face and body. Some parts you may like to look at; some you may not. But stay focused. Fight the urge to look away.

Then, after a minute or so, say aloud, *"I look in the mirror and what do I see? Whatever my defects or imperfections, I accept myself."* Say this over and over again, trying to experience the full meaning of the words.

Do this for two minutes every morning and every night for a week, and you'll begin to develop a self-acceptance about your appearance. Over time, you'll be able to set other self-acceptance goals for your behaviors, actions, attitudes, and so on.

2. Self-Worth

This is the value you place upon yourself. Self-worth asks the question: *"How important am I to myself, not to others?"*

Too often people judge themselves by what others think of them. Often this self-judgment is based on the negative opinions others hold, whether these opinions are based on truth or are part of constructive criticism. I remember a period of my life some years ago when a friend of a friend in no way disguised how much she disliked me. This person hated my clothes, the way I talked, things I did—everything about me, it seemed.

If I had felt better about myself at the time, I could've told myself, *"That's too bad she feels that way about me,"* and let it go at that. But my self-worth was low, so I tried to change myself—to become someone other than who I was—to make the other person like me. I felt I would be more worthwhile as a human being if I won this person's approval.

But self-worth means that you believe you're an important person, no matter what others feel or think about you.

The goal of developing self-worth is for you to feel that you're a valuable, important person. With a high-level of self-worth, you can believe:

- *"I'm an important person."*
- *"I know it's okay to have the things I want."*
- *"I have many good qualities."*
- *"I believe that taking care of myself is important."*
- *"I have a lot to give to myself."*

Think about this . . .

"To be nobody-but-myself—in a world which is doing its best, night and day, to make you everybody else—means to fight the hardest battle which any human being can fight, and never stop fighting."
—e.e. cummings

You can develop more self worth by creating a *Victory List*—a compilation of your successes and/or the things you've done in your life that give you great satisfaction. A victory could be major, such as leaving a bad marriage or changing jobs, or it could be a daily achievement, such as feeling pride for a job well done or making time for yourself. It doesn't matter whether the victories on your list are big or small. What matters is how good your victories make you feel. Contribute to your "Victory List" on a regular basis, and review it periodically to remind yourself that you have good qualities, that you're successful, and that you're a worthwhile human being.

3. Self-Feeling

This area of self-esteem represents how in touch you are with your feelings. The more you know about how you feel, the more aware you can be about who you are. *The goal of developing self-feeling is to identify what emotions you are experiencing at any given time.* With a high level of self-feeling, you can say:

- *"I listen to my feelings and respect them."*
- *"I'm not afraid of my feelings."*
- *"I share my feelings openly and honestly with others."*
- *"Whether I feel good or bad, I don't try to change how I feel."*

But this may be hard to do if you're not aware of *how* you feel at any given moment. It's engrained for people to respond "fine" when asked how they feel. People are often uncomfortable expressing or even feeling negative emotions such as grief, disappointment, depression, etc. Those who were raised in dysfunctional childhood homes often know how to experience only a narrow range of feelings—anxiety, anger, guilt, shame, and depression— and may have difficulty identifying other feelings.

The first step in becoming more aware of how you're feeling is to determine whether what you're feeling is a negative feeling or a positive feeling. A *negative feeling* interferes with pleasure. It uses up energy and leaves you feeling drained, empty, and alone. A *positive feeling*, on the other hand, produces pleasure. It adds to your strength and motivation and gives you a feeling of fullness, richness, and hope.

The second step in developing self-feeling is to become aware of the wide range of feelings that's your human right to experience. The FEELINGS TABLE shown on page 44 suggests some negative and positive feelings, but it's by no means a definitive list. However, you may find it helpful to consult it in identifying your feelings, especially when you keep a FEELINGS LOG, which is the third step in developing self-feeling. A FEELINGS LOG such as the one detailed on page 44 can help you get into the habit of working on your awareness about your feelings throughout the day.

Remember to be in touch with your feelings. Fill in the FEELINGS LOG by identifying how you feel when you wake up, at noontime, and before you go to bed each day for the next seven days. Use the FEELINGS TABLE to help you identify your feelings (NOTE: Not every feeling is listed; this list is designed to help you identify your emotions, if necessary.)

Think about this . . .

Surgeon Spencer Michael Free once said, *"Tis the human touch in this world that counts, the touch of your hand and mine."*

There's a story that illustrates his sentiment.

There once was a girl so afraid of people seeing her sad and lonely that she learned to excel at everything she did. She studied when others were playing so she could get good marks. She practiced sports alone trying to become the best. With all her diligent training, she earned excellent marks and made first-string softball. Everyone thought she was happy and well-adjusted. Yet she was miserable and didn't know how to say it. She had always made certain that no one touched her and no one came too close.

When you can identify your feelings, you are learning about yourself. When you can accept your feelings, you are touching yourself. When you can share your feelings, you are letting others touch you.

FEELINGS LOG

	A.M.	NOON	BEDTIME
Example:	tired, unhappy	excited, energized	quiet, lonely
Day 1.			
Day 2.			
Day 3.			
Day 4.			
Day 5.			
Day 6.			
Day 7.			

FEELINGS TABLE: *"I Feel . . ."*

NEGATIVE FEELINGS	POSITIVE FEELINGS
fearful	hopeful
anxious	serene
sad	happy
angry	peaceful
tense	calm
tired	energized
lethargic (low energy)	motivated
jealous	open-minded
suspicious	trusting
hateful	loving
rejected	supportive
ashamed	proud
lonely	connected
hurt	strong
insecure	confident
frustrated	fulfilled
guilty	secure

4. Self-Focus

This is your ability to focus on yourself, not on others. It involves putting your needs first, doing what's right for you, standing up for yourself and what you feel, and not being afraid to be yourself.

Oftentimes it's easier to focus on the needs and wants of others rather than on yourself, particularly if you don't know what you need or want, if you're used to taking care of others, if you perceive focusing on what you want or need as selfish, or if you're a "giver"—someone who doesn't always know that there's a balance in give-and-take between people.

The goal of developing self-focus is to be the master of your own life. This means you can say:

- *"I do what's right for myself."*
- *"I stand up for myself and what I feel."*
- *"I don't always do what others want me to do."*
- *"I'm not afraid to be myself."*
- *"I know it's okay to take care of my needs."*

Think about this . . .

It makes me happy to know I can make others happy. I enjoy taking care of those who are close to me. I often do what others like to do because I derive great satisfaction from their enjoyment. But when I don't listen to my needs or sacrifice what I want in order to give others what they want, then I'm not helping my self-focus.

Make a list called *21 Good Things About Me*. Write three things you like about yourself every day for a week. These things aren't what you do for others; for example, *"I like preparing a meal for a friend"* cannot be part of your list. Rather, list the qualities, actions, or behaviors you like about yourself. When you do so, you're forced to notice things about yourself. Thus, this list helps *you* focus on *you*. You may wish to fill in the list on the opposite page.

21 GOOD THINGS ABOUT ME

For the next week, list three things a day about yourself that are positive. Don't repeat any particular quality, and don't ask others what they like about you. These have to come from you! Examples:

    a. *I say what I feel.*
    b. *I eat good foods.*
    c. *I'm a dependable, loyal friend.*

1. _____
2. _____
3. _____
4. _____
5. _____
6. _____
7. _____
8. _____
9. _____
10. _____
11. _____
12. _____
13. _____
14. _____
15. _____
16. _____
17. _____
18. _____
19. _____
20. _____
21. _____

5. Self-Growth

This is your commitment to your growth, your maturation, and your ability to make changes in your life. Self-growth often involves risk-taking and goal-setting in order to make a fresh, new start.

The goal of developing self-growth is to become healthier and happier in your life. This involves making changes to achieve such health and happiness. Then you can say:

- *"I'm getting better every day."*
- *"I take risks and open up to others."*
- *"I accept and make changes in my life."*
- *"I like setting goals for myself."*
- *"I find each day challenging and exciting."*

Think about this . . .

Author A. L. Benson once remarked, *"Very often a change of self is needed more than a change of scene."*

The following five elements can help you achieve self-growth. Use them the next time you want to make a change.

The Desire to Want to Make a Change

It's one thing to say, *"I'm unhappy."* It's another thing to say, *"I'm unhappy and I want to do something about it."*

Creativity

This means opening your mind to explore and seek out new ways of doing things. This can involve reading books on a subject of interest, going for a walk on the beach to work out a plan, brainstorming ideas, listening to a motivational tape, etc.

Communication

Listen to yourself as well as receive feedback from supportive people on the changes you'd like to make in order to facilitate the process of change.

Confidence

Believe in yourself so you know you can do anything you want.

Commitment

Be committed to the changes you'd like to make so you stick with them, even when the going gets tough.

One of my students used these five elements to make a change that helped her self-growth. She told me that she often interrupted others and sometimes even tried to complete their sentences before they had finished speaking. As a result, she found that people wouldn't seek out her counsel or conversation. She desperately wanted to change (element #1—Desire) in order to become a more patient listener. So she considered ways of developing patience.

She decided one way was to count to three after someone finished speaking before she even began to reply (element #2—Creativity). She put her "patience plan" into action but went one step further. When speaking with others, she sometimes asked, *"Have I given you the opportunity to say everything you want to? Sometimes I may not realize that I've interrupted you, so please point this out to me if I do so,"* (element #3—Communication). She had designed a simple plan of action for making her change; this helped her to believe she could easily accomplish her goal (element #4—Confidence). In addition, because the plan was designed to bring about immediate results, her level of commitment was strong each time she spoke with someone (element #5—Commitment).

6. Self-Nurturing

This is your level of caring for your emotional, physical, and spiritual health and happiness. It involves taking care of yourself; treating your mind, body, and spirit well; being patient with yourself; and making choices that are right for you.

The goal of developing self-nurturing is to give kindly and lovingly to yourself. When you do, you can say:

- *"I take good care of myself."*
- *"I treat myself the way I'd like others to treat me."*
- *"I'm patient with myself."*
- *"I give love to myself."*

Think about this . . .

"Why do some people always see beautiful skies and grass and lovely flowers and incredible human beings, while others are hard-pressed to find anything or anyplace that is beautiful?" asks Leo Buscalgia. The answer lies in some people's ability to think positively and to have a bright outlook on life. People who feel good about themselves and the world around them often feel more invested in taking good care of themselves, and thus they often have a high level of self-nurturing.

Expand your positive, healing horizons in various ways to help you develop self-nurturing. Begin each day by waking up happy, for example. Sing in the shower! Dance!

When I made this suggestion to a student, the response received was a loud groan. *"I never wake up happy!"* she moaned. *"I'm always grumpy and rushed."*

"Then do something differently," I suggested. *"Change your negative routine into a positive one."*

A week later, she showed up in class with a smile on her face. *"I feel great!"* she exclaimed. *"The next morning after class, when my roommates left for work, I jumped out of my pajamas, turned on some Big Band music, picked up my cat, and danced naked in the living room with her. I've been doing that for a week. Now I can't wait for my room- mates to leave in the morning!"*

You can also develop self-nurturing by using positive self-talk from morning until night. For example, say things like *"It's another great day for me. Things are going well. I'm doing a great job."* Exercise every day, for at least 20 vigorous minutes. Laugh at least once a day. Eat nutritiously. Get plenty of rest. Stay relaxed through meditation. Play. And learn something new every day.

Do these things on a daily basis, and you'll be nurturing yourself every day!

7. Self-Guidance

This is the ability to set a course for your life. It involves becoming more independent by making decisions that are right for you.

The goal of developing self-guidance is for you to trust in your own ability to guide yourself. When you do, you can say:

- *"I know I have strength within me."*
- *"I have the wisdom and patience necessary to achieve my desires."*
- *"I make decisions for myself."*
- *"I am guided by supportive advice when I ask for it."*

Think about this . . .

> *"There are three valid answers to a yes or no question: yes, no, and no decisions right now. Eighty percent of all bad decisions are snap decisions. The best decisions are made by 'sleeping on it.'"*
>
> —Tom Parker
> Author of *Rules of Thumb*

A journal exercise called YOUR INNER VOICES can help you develop the ability to make your own decisions. Too often people are ruled by their negative, tentative, or fearful inner voices when they make decisions. They don't listen to or even allow their positive, enthusiastic inner voices to come through when considering choices that need to be made or risks that yearn to be taken.

YOUR INNER VOICES allows you to pay attention to all the "voices" that have an opinion on a particular decision. The exercise then enables you to choose which voice or voices you'll "listen" to, depending on the circumstances.

On the following page is an example of a YOUR INNER VOICES page, completed by a man who needs to decide whether to make a career change. The circled areas indicate the "voices" he chose to listen to when he made his decision.

YOUR INNER VOICES

Decision: Do I need to make a career change?

Voices	Listen To It?
"I think you ought to stay where you are."	No. Nothing will change or get better.
"You won't know anyone at the the new company."	No. I'll make friends over time.
"It'll mean more money."	Yes. I need the money.
"Your girlfriend won't like the longer hours."	No. I'll spend more time with her on the weekends.
"It will be a great opportunity and challenge."	Yes. I want to grow.

The beauty of the Inner Voices exercise is that you're making decisions that are right for you, based on how you think and what you feel. So you're not only strengthening your self-guidance with this exercise, but also your self-feeling, self-nurturing, and self-growth!

8. Self-Determination

This area of self-esteem is the grit and commitment you feel that helps you achieve what you want or need. *The goal of developing self-determination is for you to feel that who you can become is vital.* With a strong sense of self-determination, you can say:

- *"I'm always ready to make changes in my life."*
- *"I can do whatever I set out to do."*
- *"My life is filled with meaning."*
- *"Who I can become is important to me."*

Think about this . . .

"We fear to trust our wings," observes writer and metaphysician Charles B. Newcomb. *"We plume and feather them, but dare not throw our weight upon them. We cling too often to the perch."*

Begin to live your life by one rule: replace the words *"can't"* to *"can"* and *"try"* to *"will"* in your vocabulary so you eliminate words that limit your confidence and restrict your ability to be committed to making changes.

9. Self-Healing

This area of self-esteem differs from self-nurturing in that it focuses on the healing energy you have within you to combat illness and stress and to feel centered and grounded. It also encompasses your ability to have a positive attitude about yourself and how you feel inside.

The goal of developing self-healing is for you to feel good about yourself, both inside and out. Then you can say:

- *"I have a positive attitude in my life."*
- *"I treat my body with respect."*
- *"I have the power to make myself feel good."*
- *"I like how I feel inside."*

Think about this:

It is universally admitted that there is a natural healing power resident in the body. Meditation is the key to developing this self-healing. As philosopher and writer Horatio W. Dresser once remarked, *"Many people have learned to relax and keep quiet like the animals, giving nature a free opportunity to heal their maladies."*

More information about meditation will follow in the next chapter, "Health and Fitness." But an important guideline for any meditation technique you follow—exercise, taking a hot bath, being quiet, listening to a meditation tape, walking on the beach, prayer, and so on—is to do it for *a minimum of 30 minutes* three *times a week.* This will help you develop and maintain, on a regular basis, an inner connection with yourself and an outer connection with the world around you.

10. Self-Love

This area of self-esteem is the culmination of the nine other areas. Self-love is the ability to love who you are, no matter what. It works hand in hand with self-acceptance because self-love says, *"I'm not perfect, but I love myself just the way I am."*

The goal of developing self-love is for you to be able to love yourself. Then you can say:

- *"I'm not perfect, and this is comfortable."*
- *"I attract loving relationships in my life."*
- *"I feel happy with my life."*
- *"I love myself."*

Think about this . . .

I once taped the following quotation on my bathroom mirror. Every morning and night, I read the words aloud as I faced my image: *"I will love you no matter what. I will love you if you are stupid, if you slip and fall on your face, if you do the wrong thing, if you make mistakes, if you behave like a human being—I will love you no matter."*

—Leo Buscaglia

Look in the mirror every day and say out loud, *"I love you. And these are the things I love about you."* Then tell yourself *verbally* what it is you love about yourself. At first you may feel silly. You may not be able to look yourself in the eyes. But keep doing this every day. Gradually, you'll become more comfortable with your direct gaze and with expression of love for yourself.

Another method of fostering self-love is to adopt a stuffed animal. Give that stuffed animal all the positive, nurturing love you can give it: hugs, smiles, caresses, attention, play, gentleness, and kindness. Then, every day, treat yourself with the same kindness and love you show this inanimate creature!

A friend and colleague of mine is a well-known psychologist who counsels people whose friends or relatives have died suddenly. She travels frequently around the world, giving workshops and seminars to those whose lives have been touched by the somber hand of death. She's a brilliant, capable, successful professional who has developed a very high level of self-esteem—and she won't go anywhere without her traveling companion, a huge stuffed animal. This is the most pampered, loved, respected, and well-treated stuffed animal I know, but it's just like its owner. She takes as good care of herself as she does her inanimate buddy!

YOUR SELF-ESTEEM LIFEGOALS

Now write your SELF-ESTEEM LIFEGOALS. You may find the suggested "Goal Starters" helpful in creating your goals. Be sure your goals are specific to your self-esteem needs.

YOUR IMMEDIATE SELF-ESTEEM GOAL(S): to be achieved within the next few minutes to the next few hours.

GOAL STARTER: *I'm going to make my VICTORY LIST now.*

_____

_____

_____

YOUR SHORT-TERM SELF-ESTEEM GOAL(S): to be achieved within one week to one month.

GOAL STARTER: *For the next month, I'm going to focus on me by doing one good thing for myself every day.*

_____

_____

_____

YOUR MID-TERM SELF-ESTEEM GOAL(S): to be achieved within one month to one year.

GOAL STARTER: *I'm going to develop my level of self-feeling for the next six months by keeping a FEELINGS LOG and by reading the books on the READ ON list.*

_____

_____

_____

YOUR LONG-TERM SELF-ESTEEM GOAL(S): to be achieved within two to four years.

GOAL STARTER: *I'd like to take better care of myself and, at the same time, study a subject area I enjoy. I'm going to explore which colleges offer degrees in nutrition and enroll in an undergraduate program.*

_____

_____

_____

YOUR SELF-ESTEEM TARGET GOAL(S): indefinite.

GOAL STARTER: *I want to become a more relaxed, peaceful person. To achieve this end, I'd like to learn as much as I can about meditation and yoga. I'd eventually like to go on a month-long retreat to a space that offers intensive workshops on inner development.*

_____

_____

_____

READ ON

Be a Perfect Person in Just Three Days!, by Stephen Manes, a Bantam-Skylark Book, 1983.

The Book of Qualities, by J. Ruth Gendler, Harper & Row, 1984, 1988.

The Dance of Anger, by Harriet Goldhor Lerner, Ph.D., Harper & Row, 1985

Dr. Weisinger's Anger Workout Book, by Hendrie Weisinger, Ph.D., Quill, 1985.

*"Feeling Better: Nurturing Self-Esteem" (pamphlet), by Amy E. Dean, Hazelden Publishers, 1988.

How to Raise Your Self-Esteem, by Nathaniel Branden, Bantam Books, 1987.

The Language of Feelings, by David Viscott, M.D., Pocket Books, 1976.

The Power of the Plus Factor, by Dr. Norman Vincent Peale, Fleming H. Revell Co., 1987. Also, *The Power of Positive Thinking*, the classic by Dr. Peale.

Self-Defeating Behaviors, by Rebecca Curtis, Ph.D., Plenum Press, 1989.

*Books and pamphlets from Hazelden Educational Materials can be ordered by calling 1-800-328-9000.

3 □ HEALTH AND FITNESS

How You Treat Yourself

 Health and fitness is a broad category that encompasses your ability to care for your emotional, physical, and spiritual needs in order to achieve a state of well-being (health and happiness). For the purposes of this chapter, *health* is defined as your ability to combat illness and stress, and *fitness* focuses on your state of physical well-being. Both health and fitness incorporate *spiritual happiness,* which is your ability to feel connected to yourself and to the world around you.

If you're not "in touch" with your mind, body, and spiritual needs—if you're not aware of what you need to give you a sense of well-being in each of these areas nor know how to provide or obtain these needs—then you have a *weak sense of health and fitness.* People who are unaware of or who ignore basic needs such as rest, nutrition, relaxation, exercise, and peace of mind and/or choose to participate in self-destructive behaviors such as smoking, drinking to excess, taking drugs, overworking, and so on are typical of those who have a weak level of health and fitness in their lives. When I was smoking three packs of cigarettes a day, drinking caffeinated beverages, overeating, and not exercising, I clearly fell into this category.

Other people are "in touch"—aware of—their mind, body, and spiritual needs and even know how to satisfy these needs, but can't or don't consistently do so. These people have an *average sense of health and fitness.* They may go on and off diets, join health clubs, or begin exercise programs with the best intentions, but can't or don't follow through. They may feel guilty taking time off from work or putting their feet up and relaxing. They may have a low sense of self-esteem or unhealthy self-acceptance attitudes that get in the way of making a commitment to health and fitness self-improvement.

People with an average level of health and fitness seem to live lives that operate like a set of weighing scales. Sometimes the scales tip in one direction, when awareness of what their minds, bodies, and spirits need results in a great deal of attention paid to meeting these needs. One of my friends functions like this. She suddenly becomes quite obsessive about health and fitness as she plans a jam-packed weekend of activities like running, hiking, biking, and weight lifting.

Other times the scales tip in the opposite direction where, for whatever reasons, mind, body, and spiritual needs aren't met or are ignored. When my activity-obsessed friend isn't working herself into a frenzy, she's often found imitating a couch potato and griping about how much weight she's gaining and how flabby her muscles are becoming. People with an average sense of health and fitness fluctuate between not paying enough attention to themselves and caring a great deal for themselves.

But those who have a strong sense of health and fitness not only know what they need and how to provide or obtain the resources to satisfy these needs, but do so on a consistent basis. *People with a strong sense of health and fitness are emotionally, physically, and spiritually happy and healthy a majority of the time.*

In Chapter Two I said that people who have healthy self-esteem are not "at war" (in conflict) with themselves or with others. The same holds true for people who have a strong sense of health and fitness. *When emotional, physical, and spiritual health and happiness are at a high level, these people can deal with whatever challenges or difficulties life brings to them.*

YOUR MOTIVATORS

Each of the following statements reflects some of the thoughts, feelings, and behaviors of a person who has a strong sense of personal health and fitness. Do these statements accurately reflect your current sense of health and fitness?

- *"I know how to take care of myself when I don't feel well."*
- *"I'm aware of the physiological and psychological benefits of relaxation and exercise."*
- *"I play as much as possible."*
- *"I enjoy meditation and do so regularly."*
- *"I have hobbies that are important to me."*
- *"I laugh frequently."*
- *"I'm spontaneous."*
- *"I enjoy the exercise program I've designed."*

- *"Life's too short to worry about everything, so I try not to worry."*
- *"I take personal time from work when I need it."*
- *"I wake up every morning feeling motivated and energized."*
- *"When I'm sick, I allow my body to heal."*
- *"I get all the rest I need."*
- *"I'm able to handle work and family pressures with calmness and strength."*
- *"I vacation at least two weeks every year."*
- *"I'm comfortable with my free time."*
- *"I allow time for myself and what I need."*
- *"I'm organized and often prioritize my tasks."*
- *"I try to do everything in moderation."*

People who have a strong sense of health and fitness are aware of their basic needs. They eat the right foods, get plenty of rest, exercise on a regular basis, pursue outside interests, allow time for solitude as well as for socializing, and work hard to achieve a balance between responsible time (work) and relaxation (pleasure).

Although they may look in the mirror and see changes they'd like to make, overall they appreciate their bodies. They put their energy into developing their physical strength and enhancing their appearance.

If they don't feel well, they listen to their bodies and allow time to heal. They don't hesitate to seek help from those in the medical profession when their own resources offer little or no improvement. They're able to listen to others who give advice or guidance and are willing to make the changes necessary to feel better.

While they may take care of others, they make sure they take care of themselves, too. People with a strong sense of health and fitness know that self-nurturing is a necessary element in achieving inner peace and contentment. They recognize that while others may help them feel better, it's really up to them to ensure a consistent sense of well-being. As a result, they're ready to do whatever is necessary for their health and happiness.

I envy the people I know who have a strong sense of health and fitness. They seem to "fit" well with themselves. They're comfortable with their bodies, capable of expressing their feelings, and content in their moments of quiet solitude.

It's my firm belief that I take the best care of my physical, emotional, and spiritual needs when I'm relaxed, confident, and secure. But when I'm tense, under pressure, stressed out, or filled with negative energy, it becomes difficult to listen to the needs of my mind, body, and spirit. Instead, tension and negativity often take precedence.

My theory is that your ability to handle stress in your life determines your sense of health and fitness. The more capable you are of coping with stress, the stronger your sense of health and fitness will be. That's because you're able to focus more of your energy on your well-being rather than on your stress.

Let me give you an example of what I mean. Let's say

you're three days into a diet. You've lost weight and feel great. Then your boss takes an unforeseen sick leave. His assignments fall into your lap. The pressure of handling your projects as well as his builds up. Your lunchtime is disrupted, so you snack from the candy machine at work. You can't sleep at night, so you watch television and munch on sweets. Your diet gets shot to hell, not because you didn't want to stick to it, but because you couldn't cope with the stress in your life, which diverted your energy away from your diet.

In order to ensure your physical, emotional, and spiritual well-being, you need to be aware of the stresses in your life, to accept these stresses, to cope with them (handle them), and to take action to effectively deal with them.

"Your Focus" section of this chapter will provide you with a great deal of information on stress. For now, however, it's important for you to think about *where* your stress today comes from—the past or the present. Many people who have a weak or average sense of health and fitness discover that their inability to take care of their needs today is a result of the stress-related pressures they learned in their childhood. *Oftentimes what you learned in the past can cause you considerable stress today.*

The Pressures of the Past

If you were brought up in a home where there was no balance between play time and responsible time, you may find it difficult in adulthood to relax, take a vacation, or do nothing. The past messages of win, achieve, succeed, do, stay busy, make something of yourself, and so on can drive you in adulthood to feel you must work, work, work.

I remember the pressure I felt as a kid to not be sick. Perfect attendance at school was something that was rewarded; I earned the label of "model student" if I never missed a day of school. But what was the label if I happened to become ill and had to stay home?

Ignoring or not being aware of your basic human need to relax can place your physical and emotional health in jeopardy; over time, this can result in burnout, depression, anxiety, illnesses, and so on.

Another source of your stress today may be from unhealthy or self-destructive behaviors you may have learned from your parents or siblings, as you observed how they handled their personal stresses. Your father may have stopped screaming after a few beers. Your mother may have smiled after shopping. Your sister may have been easier to get along with when she ate candy. Your brother may have become kinder and more interested in your life after he smoked a few joints.

Thus, you may have learned that when you're stressed as an adult, you reach for alcohol or drugs or food or credit cards to make you feel better. (Isn't there even a saying, "When the going gets tough, the tough go shopping"?)

Finally, if you were brought up in a home where your self-esteem was destroyed through the negative messages you were told and led to believe, you may find it difficult to "tune out" such messages in adulthood. Messages like "You're no good," "You'll never amount to anything," "You'll always be fat," and so on can echo in your mind whenever you try to improve your health and happiness as an adult. One of my friends finds herself powerless to help her best friend, who has "overlost" weight—she suffers from the eating disorder known as bulimia. She grew up overweight and was constantly and critically reminded about her obesity throughout her childhood by her parents. Today she is painfully thin and close to needing hospitalization, but she can't let go of the message she heard all her life, "You're too fat." She now weighs less than 90 pounds, but still she sees herself as fat.

Negative messages from the past, even though they are no longer (or possibly were never) true, can create stress within you as you struggle to make yourself feel better in the present while your mind plays the messages over and over again, like a record with a skip on it.

It's important to recall what role your childhood may have played in influencing your ability to achieve personal health and happiness today. It's equally vital to assess everyday stresses that inhibit you from achieving a sense of well-being to determine whether they have their basis in the past.

The Pressures of Your Attitudes

Whether your stresses are based in the past, the present, or both, it can be difficult for you to raise your level of caring for your health and fitness in adulthood if you're influenced by attitudes such as the following. Do you share in any of these beliefs?

- *"I feel compulsive about work. It's what I think about from the moment I wake up until I go to bed at night."*
- *"I think it's hard to relax and have fun. That's for kids, anyway."*

- *"Meditation is a waste of time. I could be doing something, instead of just sitting around, doing nothing."*

- *"I need alcohol (drugs/food/etc.) to help me relax. A good, stiff drink after work helps me to unwind. A few drinks at a party, and I can talk to other people and have fun."*

- *"I think it's wrong to be sick. Strong people don't get sick. Weak people do."*

- *"Time demands restrict my ability to exercise. There are so many other things that I have to do, I just can't fit anything else in. Maybe when things at work (at home, in my relationship, at school, etc.) ease up, I can start running again."*

- *"I feel guilty if I'm not doing something constructive. I bring work home. I fix things around the house or clean. I take care of things other people want me to. I serve on lots of committees."*

- *"I'll diet (make time, exercise, meditate, etc.) tomorrow (Monday, next week, next year, etc.)."*

HEALTH AND FITNESS LIFEGOALS help you rise above many of these negative attitudes by making you aware of the stresses in your life, how you deal with them now, and how you can handle them more productively in the future. In addition, HEALTH AND FITNESS LIFE-GOALS help you take charge of your life and give you the opportunity to feel better physically, mentally, and spirtually.

HEALTH AND FITNESS LIFEGOALS can help you work through such common health and fitness conflicts as:

- *"How can I find the time to do everything I want to do?"*
- *"Why can't I relax?"*
- *"How do I take care of myself without ignoring my family/ lover/etc.?"*
- *"Why do I start out enthusiastically on an exercise program, then quickly lose interest?"*
- *"Am I having fun yet?"*

When you make HEALTH AND FITNESS LIFE-GOALS, you're giving yourself the opportunity *to treat yourself in a way that helps you to feel better.* This can change your life so dramatically over time that you may begin to feel like you're a different person—a healthier, happier one!

YOUR MISSION

To begin setting HEALTH AND FITNESS LIFE-GOALS, first determine the missions for your goals and outline them on the HEALTH AND FITNESS MISSIONS CHART. Your missions are based on:

1. Your particular health and fitness problem areas (Who Are You Now?);

2. What you need or want from your goals (What Do You Want to Achieve?); and

3. The type of person you'd like to become or the life you'd like to have once you achieve your goals (Who Will You Be? or How Will You Be?).

HEALTH AND FITNESS MISSIONS CHART

Who Are You Now?
Example: *I am a person who is physically out of shape.*
1. _____

_____

2. _____

_____

What Do You Want to Achieve?
Example: *I need to feel like I have more energy in order to do the things I like to do.*
1. _____

_____

2. _____

_____

Who Will You Be? or How Will You Be?
Example: *I see a person who gets up in the morning, exercises, eats a good breakfast, and goes to work a calm, centered person, able to handle the pressures of the day.*
1. _____

_____

2. _____

_____

Your Mission
Example: *I want to create a goal to begin running in the morning, every other day, for a month.*
1. _____

_____

2. _____

_____

Think about this . . .

> *"Your health is bound to be affected if, day after day, you say the opposite of what you feel, if you grovel before what you dislike, and rejoice at what brings you nothing but misfortune."*
>
> —Boris Pasternak

YOUR FOCUS

All About Health and Fitness

As I mentioned earlier, your emotional, physical, and spiritual well-being is linked directly to your ability to handle *stress*. Before you learn how to develop your physical, emotional, and spiritual sense of well-being, it's a good idea to know how to first deal with the stress that affects your ability to treat yourself well.

All About Stress

Stress is a term first used in 1946 by Hans Selye. Mr. Selye studied ways in which the body protected itself against difficulty and danger. He identified stress as *" . . . the nonspecific response of the body to any demand placed upon it . . . It is immaterial whether the agent or situation we face is pleasant or unpleasant; all that counts is the intensity of the demand for readjustment and adaptation."*

Stress can be a protector as well as a destroyer. For example, it's often thought to be the basis of many forms of illness and distress, but the stress response (fight/flight) is actually a protector. These are just two examples of the negative/positive aspects of stress. On the table below and on the following page are other examples.

STRESS: AS A DESTROYER

Some physical effects:

- increased heart rate
- headaches
- nausea/queasy stomach
- sweating

- low sex drive
- back pain
- difficulty breathing
- tightness in chest
- clenched jaw

Some emotional effects:

- anxiety
- depression
- anger
- irritability

- self-hate
- worry
- fear
- nervousness

Some spiritual effects:

- hopelessness
- lack of balance
- disrupted energy
- isolation

- inability to relax
- poor concentration
- thoughts of suicide

STRESS: AS A PROTECTOR

- Stress causes adrenalin and other chemicals to be released into the blood stream; it's an energizer.

- The pressure of stress can force some people to do their best work.

- Stress enhances the "competitive element" and can thus be a great motivator.

- Stress is a powerful force for growth; it forces people to learn and change.

- Stress energy can be harnessed and used for personal power.

Stress is a normal reaction and one that's necessary to human life: responding to stress enables you to take the actions required to keep alive and free from danger.

But while stress is normal, *tension encompasses the unpleasant physical and mental repercussions experienced when you're unable to process stress effectively.* Tension happens inside you: it's a product of how you perceive, define, and react to the world.

Processing stress effectively (eliminating the tension) involves four steps:

1. *Awareness*

2. *Acceptance*

3. *Adjustment*

4. *Action*

Before you work through these areas, find out first how well you handle stress. The quiz that follows can help you pinpoint stress areas.

HOW WELL DO YOU HANDLE STRESS?

Yes No

Awareness

☐ ☐ *Can you identify three people or situations that cause you to feel stress in your life?*

☐ ☐ *Can you list three symptoms (physical, emotional, and/or spiritual) that you suffer when you feel stress?*

Acceptance

☐ ☐ *Can you maintain a positive, calm attitude and not get upset when things don't happen the way you want them to?*

☐ ☐ *Do you believe it's okay to feel stress?*

☐ ☐ *Do you believe that everyone feels stress and that stress is part of life?*

Adjustment

☐ ☐ *When you feel stressed, can you take a "time out" and use relaxation techniques like meditation or deep breathing?*

☐ ☐ *When you feel stressed, can you exercise?*

☐ ☐ *Can you drop what you want from a stressful situation and focus on a new approach?*

Action

☐ ☐ *Do you examine your daily routine to see if you're creating stress by your habits?*

☐ ☐ *Can you express your feelings and communicate your needs during times of stress?*

☐ ☐ *Do you manage your time effectively?*

Keep your responses in mind as you explore the next four steps involved in processing stress.

Processing Stress: Keeping a STRESS LOG

The best method of developing awareness about the stresses in your life is to keep a STRESS LOG for a defined period of time: one week, two weeks, or a month. You may use the sample STRESS LOG on pages 84–85 for this purpose, or you may wish to copy the format of the STRESS LOG into a notebook.

Awareness

The *Awareness Section* of the STRESS LOG covers headings A through F.

A. Day/Time

Note the day, including the time, as you keep your LOG to help you discover patterns of your stress. One married couple that I know discovered they always argued at dinner time. That's when they both arrived home from work, had to prepare the meal, and needed to devote energy and attention to their children—a very stressful time for them. By identifying the specific time of their stress, they devised strategies to ease their transition from work to home so meal preparation time became more enjoyable and less stressful, both for them and their children.

B. Stress

In this section, list what caused you stress. Examples: *"My boss criticized my work." "I missed the train." "The furnace broke down."*

C. Classification

Determine the *types of stresses* you feel to determine the best ways to handle them.

Stresses come in many forms. Some involve *changes in lifestyle* (single to married, married to divorced, apartment living to home ownership, etc.). Some are a result of the *loss* of someone or something you cared about. Some are based on *demands or expectations* (children requiring attention, the struggle for perfection, etc.). Some are created by the *pressure of time* (deadlines and appointments). Some are from *conflict* (arguments). Some are based on *negative thoughts or attitudes* *("I don't deserve my success," "Life isn't fair," "Something bad will happen," etc.).*

Basically, stresses fall into three categories:

1. Constant pressures, which are predictable, but ongoing, such as work pressures or negative thoughts.

2. Daily hassles, such as traffic jams or juggling bathroom time in a family.

3. Episodic, which involve crises, major changes, or unplanned incidents.

No matter what types of stresses you experience in your life, understand that some are important and some are unimportant; some are controllable and some are un-controllable. *Being able to distinguish between these categories is critical not only to your awareness about stress, but also to your acceptance of what you can do about stress.* For example, if you know you can't do anything about a particular form of stress, then you can let go of your need to ''fix'' it or change it and focus on something else.

Here are examples of these four categories:

TYPES OF STRESS

Important/ controllable:	You don't like where you live. *You can look for a new place.*
Important/ uncontrollable:	Your mother is dying. *You can't make her better.*
Unimportant/ controllable:	Riding the train to work is boring. *You can buy a portable cassette player and listen to books on tape.*
Unimportant/ uncontrollable:	You think you're too short. *You can't change your height.*

D. Response—Physical Reactions

These are the physical symptoms of the stresses you experienced. For example, the stress ''My boss criticized my work'' could result in physical reactions like a nervous stomach, headache, stiff neck, and so on.

E. Response—Thoughts/Feelings

This category helps you understand your emotional responses to the stresses you experience. For example, "My boss criticized my work" could make you feel anger, humiliation, frustration, and so on.

F. Response—Actions

In this category, record what you did as a result of your stresses or in reaction to your stresses. For example, "My boss criticized my work" could have led to such actions as writing a letter of resignation, bursting into tears, yelling at your boss, asking your boss for help, and so on.

Acceptance

The *Acceptance Section* of the STRESS LOG focuses on what you would have liked to have happened as the Ideal Outcome to the stresses you have experienced.

G. Ideal Outcome

Before you write your responses in this section, first review your entries for A through F. Note any time-of-day patterns. Take stock of the kinds of things that make you feel tense and what types of stress these are. Pay attention to how your body normally responds in stressful situations—what you think or feel; how you act and react.

Then think of your responses to this statement: *"When I'm tense, I can remove that feeling and feel better by doing* _____ *."*

For the stress *"My boss criticized my work,"* you might write *"I would have liked to have asked him for specifics about his criticism rather than be immediately offended by his negativity."*

Adjustment

The *Adjustment Section* of the STRESS LOG focuses on the things you can change to help you work through your stresses more effectively the next time they occur—and possibly even eliminate the stresses from your life! Adjustment requires *you* to make the changes, or adjustments, and not to expect that other people, places, or things will change first.

H. Daily Routine Changes

Think about whether you're doing anything to contribute to your stresses. Are you hitting the snooze control button of your alarm clock so many times in the morning that you're always running behind schedule? Do you drink too much caffeine? Smoke? Don't know how to release your anger in healthy ways? Are you unable to unwind after work? Then think about the ways you can adjust your daily routine to better manage the stresses in your life.

I. Attitude Changes

This section focuses on how you can change your negative thoughts and feelings to more positive ones. For example, rather than feel defensive when your boss criticizes you, you might choose to explore why he may be under pressure and to change your own attitude as a result; for example, *"I can be more understanding of his stress because his wife is ill."*

In Attitude Changes, you might also like to write positive, affirmative statements to replace your negative attitudes. For example, rather than believe you'll always be overweight, you might choose to think, *"I'm a beautiful person who can lose weight, a little bit at a time, if I work at it."*

J. Relaxation Techniques

Being able to adjust to stress often requires the ability to be able to be calm and relaxed in the face of pressures and tensions. If you don't know how to relax, there are many resources available that outline methods such as deep breathing, meditating, and visualization techniques. Try various relaxation techniques to discover the ones you enjoy, then use them during times of stress.

K. Action

The *Action Section* of the STRESS LOG focuses on the things you can do to make your stresses more manageable. An action can include changing stressful patterns, communicating, learning how to better manage your time, asking for help from a therapist or counselor, exploring or even making changes, or setting goals. You may want to list one, two, or more actions for your stresses to demonstrate the options you have to help you handle your stresses.

Think about this . . .

Tips to Manage Your Time More Effectively

1. Make *realistic* lists of what you *can* do every day.

2. Prioritize your activities so you can work on important projects when your energy level is high and the resources are available.

3. Break bigger projects down into smaller, manageable tasks.

4. Consolidate tasks. Make all your phone calls at one time, for example. Run all your errands in a single afternoon.

5. Ask for help; delegate tasks when necessary.

6. Don't waste time. Avoid reading junk mail, for instance.

			STRESS		
AWARENESS			RESPONSE		
A. DAY/TIME	B. STRESS	C. CLASSIFICATION	D. PHYSICAL REACTIONS	E. THOUGHTS/FEELINGS	F. ACTIONS

LOG

ACCEPTANCE	ADJUSTMENT			
G. IDEAL OUTCOME	H. DAILY ROUTINE CHANGES	I. ATTITUDE CHANGES	J. RELAXATION TECHNIQUES	K. ACTION

Think about this . . .

"My relationship with fitness had been one of struggle, starvation, self-abuse, and discomfort . . . I acted as if fitness, success, and self-abuse were synonymous. Although I taught that there is no gain in pain, I lived, until that time, a 'no gain, no pain' existence."

"I learned that my belief system created my reality. You create a new relationship with your body if you listen to it, love it, honor it, and enjoy it. It is possible to look at your body and to find things you like about it, and to find ways that your body serves your life."

—Suzy Prudden
Author of *MetaFitness*

Physical: The Power to Strengthen Your Body

A study led by Dr. John Ragland in the sports pyschology laboratory at the University of Wisconsin (Madison) revealed that reduced stress levels lasted only 20 minutes after 40 minutes of rest, *but lasted three hours after 40 minutes of aerobic exercise!* It's vital, for your physical health, that you exercise vigorously at least 20 minutes every day. The purpose of such exercise—an overall sense of physical well-being—combines four areas: weight control, heart disease prevention, fitness, and an antidote to stress.

You may choose one exercise or sport or opt for the

whole-body benefit of cross-training. *Cross-training is the combination of two or more routines that complement each other.* For example, runners do little with their upper bodies, so swimming or weight lifting would be good cross-training choices. The proliferation of health clubs as well as affordable home gym set-ups have made cross-training more accessible. But the purpose of this chapter is not to focus on what types of exercise programs to choose from, but on how to make an exercise program work.

When you set your exercise program goals, keep these guidelines in mind.

• *Discuss your ability to exercise and any problems that you need to be aware of with a medical doctor.* I have exercise-induced asthma, but it doesn't limit my running, even in cold weather, because of the medical treatment provided by my allergist.

• *Discuss an exercise program and any health limits you have with a professional trainer, physical fitness instructor, or physical therapist.* Often these people can design and/or recommend a fitness program that's tailored to fit your specific needs.

When I acquired "tennis elbow" one summer, I thought I had to give up all activities that involved motion in my arm. But a physical therapist provided me with a treatment plan for rehabilitating my elbow and also gave me an outline of activities I could still participate in.

• *Keep in mind that an exercise program can include a workout-style regimen as well as vigorous activity designed for pleasure; for example, hiking with friends, horseback riding, walking on the beach, canoeing, planting a garden, or simply walking.*

- *Remember to make your fitness goals realistic and easy to achieve.* When I first began weight lifting, I felt ashamed to be lifting such a small amount of weights, especially when those around me in the gym were straining under considerably larger amounts of weight. But I made my weight lifting goals incremental so I could gradually build up my weights over time.

- *Allow for a time of congratulation/celebration when you make your goal.* When I first started running, I didn't do this. Instead, once I achieved a five-mile goal I went immediately to a six-mile goal, then to a seven-mile goal, then to an eight-mile goal. As a result, I burned out quickly and gave up running after a short time. It was years before I began running again; then, it was for pleasure.

- *Learn how your body works by "listening" to it.* Are you more energetic in the morning? afternoon? evening? Do you like exercises that work your legs? shoulders? back? Arms? Gear your exercise program to your high-motivation times and to the exercises your body likes the most.

- *Examine the motives for your exercise program.* Ask yourself: *"What do I want from exercising?"* Examine your answers: *"To lose weight." "To strengthen my heart." "To feel better."* Then ask yourself: *"Will my exercise program help me achieve what I want?"*

- *Choose an exercise you like.* To find one, ask: *"What kind of activity do I like the most? Why? Why am I not doing it now? Can I still do it? Or is there a good substitute?"*

- *Dress for success.* It's often recommended that you don't spend a lot of money on clothes or equipment when you're just starting out on an exercise program. But that's not my belief. I like to look good and feel like I have the best equipment or clothing for the activity. If I don't, I can always use those as excuses for quitting. When people tell me, "My feet hurt, so I stopped running," I ask them what type of shoes they bought. More often than not, they purchased a bottom-line shoe or a non-running shoe. So it's no wonder their feet hurt!

• *Make a reward system that "earns" you something for your successful efforts—a new outfit, relaxation time in the sauna, taking an afternoon to watch a sports event on television, and so on.*

• *If possible, share your exercise program with a friend so you have someone to run with, swim with, play tennis with, and so on.*

• *Don't give yourself room to quit.* For example, lay out your exercise clothes the night before so they're ready in the morning.

Think about this . . .

"The truth that many people never understand, until it is too late, is that the more you try to avoid suffering the more you suffer because smaller things begin to torture you in proportion to your fear of suffering."

—Thomas Merton

Emotional: The Power to Strengthen Your Mind

There are three areas that are critical to developing your emotional well-being in the present: recovering from past emotional hurts, building self-esteem, and learning about the healing power in play and laughter.

Past emotional hurts can cause a lifetime of pain and can create a great deal of daily inner tension. The best way to deal with these hurts in the present is to try to resolve your feelings about them through options such as *therapy*, which can help you uncover and discover issues from the past in order to recover from them in the present; *building your self-esteem*, which was discussed in Chapter Two; *keeping a journal*, in which you record your feelings; *working on forgiveness*, in which you try to think differently about the situation in order to resolve the hurt; and *recognizing what you can change in your life and what you can't change*.

The prayer used by members of Alcoholics Anonymous is a great tool that helps me work through my emotional pain of the past:

"God grant me the serenity to accept the things I cannot change, Courage to change the things I can, and the Wisdom to know the difference."

You may wish to set goals for your emotional well-being based on one or more of these suggestions.

Also, the healing power of laughter and play can have a significant impact in helping you strengthen your mind. Here are the reasons why:

First, laughter and play help you cope. They draw attention away from your problems, if only for a moment. They can also help diffuse stressful situations and release tension. When I was invited to spend Christmas with friends whose father was dying of bone cancer, they said, "Amy, we can use your sense of humor. It'll make things easier for us."

They were so focused on illness, their powerlessness, and the impending loss of their father that they couldn't get outside their sorrows. But when we got together on Christmas day, I talked about how much fun I had had with their family during the vacations and holiday weekends we had spent together. We started reminiscing, and soon we were laughing and talking about all the happy times we had shared.

Second, laughter and play keep you balanced when they're combined with responsible time. Then you're not focused only on serious, adult issues, but also on playful, childlike activities. I used to be very compulsive about my yard work, especially in autumn when the leaves began to fall. I'd rake for hours on the weekends, creating massive piles of leaves. Then I'd invariably strain my back hauling the leaves away. I viewed raking the leaves as a necessary chore of the adult homeowner.

Then one of my friends helped me rake one Saturday. As soon as we had created a massive pile of leaves, he dropped his rake, raced across the yard, threw his arms in the air, let out a yell, then charged straight for the pile. He leaped and landed in it, disappeared for a moment, then poked his head out, looked at me, and started laughing.

I was dumbstruck. I thought, "All that hard work, and

now we have to rake some more!" But then I thought, "You know, I've never jumped in a pile of leaves. I wonder what it feels like." So I dropped my rake, aimed straight for the pile, and dove in. What a thrill! I had never really smelled the leaves before nor tossed them above me and watched them float down on my face.

That day, raking leaves was one heck of a lot of fun!

Third, laughter and play provide you with perspective. Play and laughter can make your larger upsets seem smaller, can expand your limited picture, and can get you to see more than your own problems and pressures.

I remember one Christmas season I bought myself one of those cheap plastic strips kids use to sled on. I walked to the local golf course on a bright, sunny, school vacation day and watched the kids slide down the hill. As I stood there, I focused on one little girl who was quite determined to race up the hill after every run down so she could get the most out of the perfect sledding day.

I eventually became friendly with her. She explained to me how to have the best run down the hill—a run that included every bump and dip in the hill and added the most speed. She raved about how "neat" and "excellent" and "awesome" and "cool" the rides down the hill were. I couldn't help but get caught up in her excitement, energy, and wild abandon. I wanted to race down that hill!

So I grit my teeth and battled for ten minutes trying to get the damn plastic strip to lay flat on the ground.

That accomplished, I flopped down on my plastic strip—which, I ought to mention, offers no protection between the hill and the base of your spinal column and the major bones in your body—and I went on a teeth-rattling, wind-chilling, internal-organ-jarring ride of my life.

As I shot down the hill at top speed and headed for a sharp dip, my eyes blurred from the cold wind. But I was well aware of the curl that would greet me as I flew out of the dip—a curl that would make me airborne.

At that moment, I wasn't thinking about anything "adult."

I wasn't thinking about what I was making for dinner that night or whether my insurance policy was up to date (although I did flash for a second on seeing myself laid up in a bed, in traction, for about three months). I didn't think about car payments or business clients—or even if I was going to die.

Instead, I just wanted to laugh.

And I laughed as I shot out of the dip, into the quick curl, and into the air.

I lost my grip on the plastic strip and landed where an eight-pack of quilted Northern bathroom tissue would have felt great.

My little friend met me at the bottom of the hill.

I stared up at her from my spread-eagle position on the ground, where I had stopped when the hill had mercifully ended.

"Excellent!" she said. "Race you to the top!"

That one day changed my perspective on life and made me realize how little laughter and play I had allowed myself to experience.

Later on that night, as I soaked in a hot tub, I felt relaxed in a way I never had before in my life.

I felt like a kid.

And I was happy.

Think about this . . .

Tips to Learn How to Play and Laugh

1. Be with children and play with them or observe them playing. See their complete lack of inhibition and self-criticism.

2. Laugh for the pure pleasure of laughing. Watch comedy shows, listen to comedy records or tapes, read joke books, and so on.

3. Find yourself a "buddy"—someone to have fun with—who you trust fully and have no fear of being judged or rejected by.

4. Look at the world through a child's eyes. Marvel at the wonders of the world, both big and small, from the space shuttle to an ant hill.

5. Read children's books for their freshness and humor.

6. Play non-competitive games with yourself and others.

7. Every day, do something different, spontaneous, and playful.

8. Keep in mind the definition of play—it's light-hearted activity that has no apparent purpose. With play, you lose yourself in the fun of the moment and relax your mind and body. Do you play?

Spiritual: The Power to Strengthen Your Spiritual Connection

The best way to develop your connection with yourself and the world around you is to give yourself time for solitude, time in which you pay attention to your "voices" within. At least 30 minutes of solitude a day helps reduce stress and renew your energy for difficult situations.

In this time, you can relax, read, write, reminisce, plan, meditate, think, or dream. This is the time to clear the "debris" out of your mind—negative thoughts, expectations, pressures, and so on—and focus on positive things—achievements, "magic moments," nice memories, and calm scene.

During this time, your mind and body don't need to be totally relaxed. Just give yourself the space to be comfortable and quiet. Let the thoughts in your mind flow freely, without processing any of them.

When you develop your spiritual well-being, you're recharging your batteries—giving yourself the opportunity for a fresh start, new energy, or a different outlook.

The "Read On" section at the end of this chapter lists written and audio materials to help you develop your spiritual well-being. You might like to try at least two to experience different techniques. In addition, Chapter Eight discusses how to connect your physical and emotional nature to the development of spiritual understanding.

YOUR HEALTH AND FITNESS LIFEGOALS

Now write your HEALTH AND FITNESS LIFE-GOALS. You may find the suggested "Goal Starters" helpful in creating your goals. Be sure your goals are specific to your health and fitness needs.

YOUR IMMEDIATE HEALTH AND FITNESS GOAL(S): to be achieved within the next few minutes to the next few hours.

GOAL STARTER: *I'm going to start my Stress Log today.*

_____

_____

_____

YOUR SHORT-TERM HEALTH AND FITNESS GOAL(S): to be achieved within one week to one month.

GOAL STARTER: *I want to start and continue my running program for one month.*

_____

_____

_____

YOUR MID-TERM HEALTH AND FITNESS GOAL(S): to be achieved within one month to one year.

GOAL STARTER: *I'm going to join Weight Watchers and design a diet that will help me lose 50 pounds this year.*

_____

_____

_____

YOUR LONG-TERM HEALTH AND FITNESS GOAL(S): to be achieved within two to four years.

GOAL STARTER: *I'm going to begin a weight lifting program and a nutrition plan, with the desire of entering competitive body building events in two years.*

YOUR HEALTH AND FITNESS TARGET GOAL(S): indefinite.

GOAL STARTER: *I'm going to begin a meditation program and become a more relaxed, calmer person.*

READ ON

Changing Your Life, by Strephon Kaplan-Williams, MFCC, Journey Press, 1987.

Creative Visualization, by Shakti Gawain, Whatever Publishing, Inc., 1986.

Healers on Healing, edited by Richard Carlson, Ph.D. and Benjamin Shield, Jeremy P. Tarcher, Inc., 1989.

The Healing Power of Humor, by Allen Klein, Jeremy P. Tarcher, Inc., 1989.

Heal Your Body, by Louise L. Hay, Hay House, Inc., 1984.

How to Find a Good Psychotherapist, by Judi Striano, Ph.D., Professional Press, 1987.

Life! You Wanna Make Something of It?, by Dr. Tom Costa, Hay House, Inc., 1988.

The Massage Book, by George Downing, Random House, constantly updated.

MetaFitness: Your Thoughts Taking Shape, by Suzy Prudden and Joan Meijer-Hirschland, Hay House, Inc., 1989.

Natural Home Remedies, by Mark Bricklin, Rodale Press, 1982.

Peace, Love, and Healing, by Dr. Bernie Siegel, Harper & Row, 1989.

The People's Guide to Vitamins and Minerals: From A to Zinc, by Dominick Bosco, Contemporary Books, Inc., 1980.

The Relaxation and Stress Reduction Handbook, by Martha David, Ph.D.; Matthew McKay, Ph.D.; and Elizabeth Robbins Eshelman, M.S.W.; New Harbinger Publications, 1982.

Self-Health Guide, by Kripalu Center for Holistic Health, Box 120, Summit Station, PA, 1980.

Self-Renewal, by Dennis T. Jaffe, Ph.D. and Cynthia D. Scott, Ph.D., M.P.H., Simon & Schuster Inc., 1984.

Take a Deep Breath, by Dr. James E. Loehr and Dr. Jeffrey A. Migdow, Villard Books, 1986.

Vegetarian Medicines, by Clarence Meyer, Meyerbooks, IL, 1981.

Yoga for All Ages, by Rachel Carr, Simon & Schuster, 1972.

You Can Heal Your Life, by Louise L. Hay, Hay House, Inc.,1984.

Your Erroneous Zones, by Dr. Wayne W. Dyer, Funk & Wagnalls, 1976.

The Well Body Book, by Mike Samuels, M.D. and Hal Bennett, Random House, constantly updated.

Working Inside Out: Tools for Change, by Margo Adair, Wingbow Press, 1984.

Relaxation Tapes

"Creative Visualization," by Shakti Gawain, Whatever Publishing, Inc., P.O. Box 137, Mill Valley, CA 94942.

"Environments" series, Syntonic Research, Inc., 175 Fifth Avenue, New York, NY 10010.

"Solitudes" series, by Dan Gibson Productions Ltd., The Moss Music Group Inc., 48 West 38th Street, New York, NY, 10018.

"Working Inside Out," by Margo Adair, Wingbow Press, Book People, 2929 Fifth Street, Berkeley, CA 94710.

4 □ RELATIONSHIPS

How You Interact With Others

 *A **relationship** is your connection with any people who have a reason to be in your life, including friends, business associates, group affiliations, social contacts, and love or sexual interactions.* This connection can be unhealthy, immature, or healthy.

An unhealthy relationship is based on some level of fear, doubt and/or insecurity. These feelings can be exhibited in some of the following ways: fear of abandonment, fear of dependency, fear of intimacy, fear of losing control; lack of trust, lack of faith, jealousy, possessiveness, lying; fusion (unhealthy bonding in which two people act, think, and respond as one person), lack of individuality, low self-esteem, lack of personal growth, excessive caretaking; and so on. In an unhealthy relationship, such feelings are often predominant and can influence the relationship in negative ways.

For example, one or both of the partners may feel depressed or unhappy a good deal of the time. Or, one may be threatened by the other's interests and achievements, even if such things help that person feel happy or fulfilled. An unhealthy relationship can include selfish, rude, or abusive behavior, with one person thinking or acting without regard to the other's feelings.

People in an unhealthy relationship may be unaware of the behaviors in the relationship, or they may know the relationship is unhealthy but may have difficulty making changes due to their own fears, doubts, and insecurities. A few years ago, one of my friends used to call me at least once a week to complain about things her boyfriend said, did, didn't say, or didn't do. I finally asked her why she stayed with him. She thought for a moment, then replied, "I don't know."

An immature relationship is one that has the potential to become a healthy relationship because one or both of the partners are willing to work or are working on becoming happier, healthier people. An immature relationship may have its faults and difficulties, but the people in it are receptive to doing whatever is necessary to make it work. This process may involve individuals making personal changes, with the ultimate goal of feeling better about themselves (dieting, going to therapy, spending time alone, learning something new or pursuing hobbies or other interests, dealing with an addiction, and so on).

It may also entail both people working together to identify, confront, and take action on issues that adversely affect the relationship, with the ultimate goal of making it healthier (improving communication skills, scheduling time to spend together as well as apart, working out a household budget, equally dividing household tasks, and so on). An immature relationship can be a new or established relationship that's reached a healthier stage of growth.

A healthy relationship is one in which the two people are supportive and geared toward developing the qualities of trust, honesty, a sense of individuality, nurturing, and knowledge (awareness) about the themselves and their relationship.

While the partners in a healthy relationship may feel fear, doubt, and insecurity from time to time, they can work through these feelings by maintaining open and honest communication, by confronting important issues, by being willing to compromise or see the other's point of view, and by developing a sense of commitment to individual growth as well as to the growth of the relationship. Healthy relationships resolve conflict, build respect, develop intimacy, have a sense of direction and purpose, and remain fresh and ever-changing over time. In a healthy relationship, the people involved feel good about themselves as well as about the relationship.

Think about this . . .

What Love Really Means

A teacher in an adult education writing class instructed her students to write "I love you" in 25 words or less, without using the words "I love you." One woman in the class contributed the following:

"Why, I've seen lots worse hairdos than that, honey."

"These cookies are hardly burned at all."

"Cuddle up—I'll get your feet warm."

—Charlotte Mortimer,
contributed to *Reader's Digest*

YOUR MOTIVATORS

Each of the following statements reflects some of the thoughts, feelings, and behaviors of someone who is involved in a healthy relationship. Do these statements accurately reflect who you are and how you feel in your current relationships?

- *"I don't change who I am for others."*
- *"I pursue my own interests and encourage others to do the same."*
- *"I accept others for who they are, without trying to control or change them."*
- *"I communicate openly and honestly about what I need and how I feel."*
- *"I'm not afraid to be intimate."*
- *"I trust others."*
- *"I'm not afraid to be vulnerable."*
- *"I like to give as well as to receive."*
- *"My relationships enrich my life."*
- *"I'm passionate with others."*
- *"I can discuss sensitive issues."*
- *"My relationships are continually growing and changing."*
- *"I'm not afraid to experience new people, places, or things."*
- *"I enjoy physical and emotional closeness."*
- *"I share who I am with others."*
- *"I like making plans and setting goals with others."*

- *"I don't have expectations of others."*
- *"I'm not afraid to be in a committed relationship."*

Healthy relationships are made up of two individuals who, no matter how similar they may be, know how important it is to grow separately as well as to grow within the boundaries of the relationship. Because of this, those in a healthy relationship accept one another's good qualities as well as the bad. They encourage and support issues and ideals that are important to one another, and they aren't threatened by time spent apart. Because they accept each other for who they are, there's usually little or no dominance, control, or manipulation of another to effect changes.

Instead, there's open and honest communication. People in healthy relationships aren't afraid to discuss sensitive areas that involve issues such as money, sex, inequality, or imbalance in the relationship, individual needs as well as the needs of the relationship, expectations, and the future. Those in healthy relationships consider communication to be the key that unlocks the doors of awareness to one another as they interact within the relationship. In addition, in healthy relationships people share all feelings verbally, the good as well as the bad, and an acceptance of these shared feelings.

A healthy relationship also involves nurturing others when it's possible and appropriate to their growth. That means that those in a healthy relationship don't become overly dependent on each other, don't expect someone else to make them happy, and don't presume that someone will solve all their problems. Healthy relationships have healthy nurturing—an equal balance of giving and receiving.

Those in a healthy relationship are willing to be intimate with each other and to share love. They're not afraid to experience physical closeness as well as to show their love and trust for each other. In healthy relationships, people bond with each other, talk about their feelings, establish a level of honest communication, and work together to solve problems and resolve conflicts.

Healthy relationships are satisfying and fulfilling to the people involved.

The first relationship you have is with your mother and father. *This relationship sets the parameters for many of the relationships you form in adulthood.*

If dysfunction existed in your childhood home, the focus was most likely placed on the dysfunction and/or on the parent(s) who was dysfunctional (alcoholic, abusive, workaholic, chronically ill, etc.). When this happened, attention to you, your siblings, and even to the other parent may have become secondary.

You may have learned, then, that sacrifices are made in relationships, sacrifices that include such things as time limitations or lack of communication. Your needs may have been ignored. You may have had little or no consistency in feeling secure in your relationships with your parents. You may have been given mixed messages ("You matter to me. Get lost.") that affected your ability to develop confidence and trust in feelings expressed by others. One student in my class related to me how difficult it is for him to hear his girlfriend say she loves him. He explained why.

"When I was growing up, I didn't get a lot of attention

from my parents. I often felt alone. One day I sat down next to my mother on the couch. She was reading a magazine. 'Mom, do you love me?' I asked. Without even looking up from her reading, she answered, 'Do I have any reason to?' After that, I told myself I'd never believe anyone who said they loved me."

But even if your parents weren't dysfunctional, they could have still been unhealthy role models when it comes to relationships. For example, parents who say they'll be there and then aren't—emotionally as well as physically—may lead their children to believe that they'll be abandoned in relationships or may teach them not to trust the actions and words of others. Parents who express love at the same time that they're being sexually, physically, or verbally abusive may show their children that being loved means being hurt. These children may then form relationships in adulthood with people who perpetuate those same behaviors.

Children who are urged to be "grown up" and responsible "adults" in their childhood homes—perhaps by taking care of the needs of both siblings and parents or by performing duties normally undertaken by those at a much older age—may form relationships with people in adulthood who are insecure and who need to be taken care of.

Children who experience inconsistent guardianship while growing up may have difficulty making commitments to anyone in adulthood, believing instead that any relationship they form will be temporary anyway. Or they may become "clinging vines" in their relationships, fearful of separation or of pursuing individual interests because they believe they'll be left alone.

Earlier I related the circumstances of my own child-hood—being adopted into an alcoholic home, spending time in a foster home, and having four mothers by the time I was seven years old. Needless to say, it's been a struggle for me to learn and to accept that relationships allow for times of separation—and that these times aren't necessarily signals of impending abandonment!

Think about this . . .

> _"Let's face it, relationships are tough,"_ com-ments actress Meredith Baxter Birney, of the popular television series, _Family Ties. "They are so multifaceted. You just have to be open to anything and be willing to fight for them. I didn't know that when I first married. I was very young. It also helps if you have a lot of good role models around you, and that was not necessarily the case for me."_

Whatever messages you were given in your childhood about relationships comprise the blueprints you use in build-ing your relationships as an adult. The healthier your parents' relationship with each other was and your rela-tionship was with them, the healthier your relationships will most likely be in adulthood.

It's important, then, in your relationship goal setting, to reflect on what you learned about relationships as a child. Think about how you were shown love and how your parents expressed love for each other. Then reflect on your responses to these questions:

Did your parents have separate interests? Were they

allowed to pursue these interests without creating conflict? Did they encourage you to develop friendships and hobbies? Did they support you in new endeavors? Did they encourage open, honest communication and effectively resolve conflicts with each other and their children? Did they express physical affection towards each other and their children by hugs, kisses, or nonsexual, nonthreatening touch? How did your parents make you feel about your ability to love and to be loved?

Next look at SIGNS OF HEALTHY/UNHEALTHY RELATIONSHIPS. To determine whether your relationship(s) are unhealthy, immature, or healthy, answer the following questions yes or no. Add up the number of yes responses in each list.

SIGNS OF HEALTHY/UNHEALTHY RELATIONSHIPS

Unhealthy Cues

_____ Do you ignore your own feelings, but feel another's feelings very intensely?

_____ Do you rescue others rather than offer support?

_____ Do you take orders from others or do things even when you don't want to?

_____ Do you agree with others to avoid conflict?

_____ Do you have sex to please your partner?

_____ Do you adapt to the needs, wants, or expectations of others?

_____ Do you give, give, give?

_____ Do you blame yourself for the behaviors of others or for the conflicts in your relationship(s)?

_____ Do you believe others will be strong for you?
_____ Do you expect one person to provide all your emotional needs?
_____ Do you expect others to meet your needs, whether or not you communicate these needs?
_____ Do you manipulate or try to control others?
_____ Do you feel unequal in your relationship(s)?
_____ Are you mistrustful of others?
_____ Are you obsessed with finding someone to love?
_____ Do you pressure others for long-term commitment before you really get to know them?
_____ Do you process conflict by fighting or not talking?
_____ Do you believe others (or love) will make you happy?
_____ Do you doubt your relationship(s) can change for the better?
_____ Do you apologize frequently for your behavior?
_____ Do you often feel anger or resentment in your relationship(s)?
_____ Do you often feel insecure in your relationship(s)?
_____ Do you often feel drained or exhausted in your relationship(s)?
_____ Do you expect to have or to find the perfect lover?
_____ Do you believe you don't deserve love?

_____ **TOTAL (out of 25)**

Healthy Cues

_____ Do you often feel secure in your relationship(s)?
_____ Do you often trust others?
_____ Do you feel relaxed in your relationship(s)?

_____ Do you like who you are in relationships?

_____ Do you know you have many good things to share with others?

_____ Do you feel beautiful and lovable?

_____ Do you think you're trustworthy in your relationships?

_____ Can you love someone else?

_____ Are your needs being met by many people, not by just one or two?

_____ Are you open and honest with yourself and others?

_____ Do you communicate your feelings to others?

_____ Do you accept others as individuals?

_____ Do you appreciate your qualities as well as the qualities of those around you?

_____ Can you be yourself with others?

_____ Do you let others see who you really are?

_____ Do you desire relationships with good and healthy people?

_____ Do you bring good qualities into your relationships?

_____ Do you let others give you love and care?

_____ Do you feel blessed by your wonderful relationships?

_____ Are you patient in your relationships; do you know they'll develop gradually?

_____ Are you aware of your freedom of choice in your relationships?

_____ Can you resolve conflict in your relationships?

_____ Do you feel content and peaceful around others?

_____ Can you compromise or negotiate with others?

_____ **TOTAL (out of 25)**

If the majority of your yes responses were in the UN-HEALTHY CUES list, then your relationship(s) are probably unhealthy. You may find the information in YOUR FOCUS beneficial to improving the quality of your relationship(s).

If the majority of your yes responses were in the HEALTHY CUES list, then your relationship(s) are probably healthy. You may wish to set RELATIONSHIP LIFE-GOALS that refine your current interactions by helping you progress to a deeper level of intimacy with others.

If your yes responses were almost evenly split between the two lists, then your relationship(s) are probably immature. To ensure that your relationship(s) develop into healthy ones, you may find the information in YOUR FOCUS beneficial in setting RELATIONSHIP LIFEGOALS.

Think about this . . .

"Romance isn't always pretty dresses and guys that don't sweat. Sometimes it's about threat and anxiety and fear and walking through minefields together."
—Actor James Woods

RELATIONSHIP LIFEGOALS can help you improve the quality of your interactions with others while, at the same time, teach you much about who you are and what you need in your relationships. While RELATIONSHIP LIFEGOALS may not make all your relationships more satisfying and fulfilling, they can help you change some for the better and/or lead you to form new, exciting relationships with people you might not have let yourself get to know.

RELATIONSHIP LIFEGOALS can help you work through such common relationship issues as:

- *"How can I resolve conflicts more effectively?"*
- *"How can I develop a more equal balance of give-and-take with others?"*
- *"In what ways can I learn to trust others?"*
- *"What is intimacy and how can I learn to open up more?"*
- *"What should I look for in my maturing relationships?"*

When you make RELATIONSHIP LIFEGOALS, you're giving yourself the opportunity to develop the qualities needed to make your relationships healthy. When you make improvements in your relationships, you're saying to yourself and to others: *I can give love and I can be loved.*

YOUR MISSION

To begin setting RELATIONSHIP LIFEGOALS, first determine a few missions for your goals and outline them on the RELATIONSHIPS MISSIONS CHART. Your missions are based on:

1. Your particular relationship problem areas (Who Are You Now?);

2. What you need or want from your goals (What Do You Want to Achieve?); and

3. The type of person you'd like to become or the life you'd like to have once you achieve your goals (Who Will You Be? or How Will You Be?).

RELATIONSHIPS MISSIONS CHART

Who Are You Now?
Example: *I am a person who finds it difficult to think of my own needs in an intimate relationship.*
1. _____
_____
2. _____
_____

What Do You Want to Achieve?
Example: *I want to be able to do things apart from my lover and not feel like I'm thinking only of me.*
1. _____
_____
2. _____
_____

Who Will You Be? or How Will You Be?
Example: *I see myself as a happier, more content person in my relationship with my lover.*
1. _____
_____
2. _____
_____

Your Mission
Example: *I want to create a goal that will allow me to take one night a week apart from my lover to do whatever I want.*
1. _____
_____
2. _____
_____

YOUR FOCUS

All About Relationships

In the beginning of this chapter I mentioned the five components of a healthy relationship: trust, honesty, individuality, nurturing, and knowledge. To bring about positive changes in your relationships through goal-setting, it's helpful to recognize how each of these components affects your interactions with others and how to develop them in your relationships.

Think about this . . .

> *"We've been together 13 years. She's my best friend. She's the one person I can trust completely. I have friends that I trust 100 percent. I trust her 105 percent."*
> —NBA basketball player Larry Bird about his wife, Diane Mattingly

---

1. Trust

The first and most important element of any healthy relationship is trust. Even if you have the four other components in your relationships, your interactions won't be strong and positive without developing a certain level of trust.

Trust is the basis of belief, faith, and confident reliance on someone's character, honesty, or strength. It's believing that someone is going to be physically and emotionally dependa-

ble. In relationships, trust comes from two areas: trust in oneself and trust in others.

Trust in oneself is based first on always doing what you say you're going to do. After all, if you don't believe in your own words or actions, then it's going to be hard to depend upon yourself. And if you let yourself down, imagine how hard it's going to be for others to trust in you!

Trust in yourself is also based on the confidence in your ability to distinguish the "safe" people from the "unsafe" people in your life.

"Unsafe" people are unhealthy. They're angry, critical, withdrawn, abusive, overwhelming, exhausting, negative, depressed, demanding, manipulative, and run hot and cold. "Safe" people are loving, supportive, helpful, kind, positive, encouraging, consistent, nurturing, honest, understanding, and self-satisfied. Safe people are healthy or are working towards becoming healthier.

By learning to distinguish between the two types of people, you can make conscious choices in your interactions with others: to choose to be with people who treat you well and who can meet some of your needs, or to be with those who will make great demands upon you for their own benefit. Unsafe people will drain you; safe people will energize you.

The goal of developing trust in yourself is to learn how to listen to your intuitive side—your "gut feel"—about people and situations and to ask yourself whether your needs can be met by these people. Believe what you can see, hear, sense, and touch; don't believe what's not there.

Trust in others begins when you create a small, but firm foundation where you identify at least one person in your life who's consistently caring and conscientious. The key word is *consistent*. The term "fair weather friends" was created for a reason: to identify those who can be there when the times aren't tough, when the demands upon them aren't great.

A friend of mine found this term to hold true when she had to take care of her mother, who was diagnosed with inoperable cancer and given only weeks to live. It was at that time that my friend really needed the support of her friends; it was also then that she discovered which friends she could rely upon, which ones she could trust.

The ones she could trust were those people who, day in and day out, wanted to help her through her difficult time. Those were the people who remained consistent in their caring and actions. The friends she couldn't trust were those who begged off from helping her by offering a multitude of excuses, who showed impatience or dealt with her feelings abruptly, and who rarely called to show they cared.

However, my friend was fortunate in that she had a small, firm foundation of people she could trust. She wasn't alone during this difficult period of her life.

Developing trust in others doesn't mean asking someone to jump off a bridge for you or waiting until you have a dying parent to see who can help you through such an intensely emotional time. Developing trust means starting small, perhaps by asking someone to pick you up from work and drive you home when your car is in the shop. Or it can be starting a conversation with a person who shares something in common with you. One of my closest friendships with a coworker began by discussing how much we loved a particular brand of chocolate chip cookie, which could only be found in his home state. Thereafter, whenever he went home for holidays or vacations, he always brought me back a box of those delicious treats. Over time, our friendship grew as we shared more about ourselves, our likes, dislikes, wants, and needs. Today he is one of my dearest friends, someone on whom I can rely.

The goal of establishing a small, but firm foundation of trust in others is to become more open and, as a result, to develop intimacy, which is simply a deeper level of trust.

Intimacy begins with openness. Openness has two definitions:

1. It's the appropriate sharing of facts, feelings, attitudes, and points of view. *This often leads to intimacy.*

2. It's the willingness to risk exposure to new ideas and new experiences. *This often leads to change and growth.*

Openness is part of the process of getting closer to people. Openness requires that you release some of the emotional and physical protective barriers that surround you in order to let others get to know you better. By opening up to others, you can work through a fear like: *"If he/she only knew me, then he/she wouldn't like me."* Openness helps build bridges to others so you won't be alone in good times or hard times. And openness leads to better planning, thinking, and problem-solving with others because the more information you have about those around you and the more information they have about you, the more capable you and others will be in making decisions that are right for your relationships.

The goal of being open is to develop intimacy (emotional closeness) and to be receptive to experiencing change and growth with others.

Think about this . . .

"The easiest kind of relationship for me is with ten thousand people. The hardest is with one."
—singer Joan Baez

It's often difficult to know when to open up, who to open up to, and just how much to reveal. But here are some questions and comments that can help you make such decisions.

• **ASK YOURSELF:** *"Is what I'm about to share acceptable for this person to know right now?"*

Too often people share intimate details of their lives within the first few weeks of knowing someone. Or they offer information that may be inappropriate or unacceptable for someone to know; for example, telling someone who's anxious about an upcoming operation details of gruesome hospital stays.

• **ASK YOURSELF:** *"Is this person able to handle this information?"*

Keep in mind how capable the other person is to receive the information you share. There are times when I've chosen to withhold information for a while due to another person's personal stress, a differing background, or lack of information about a particular topic. For example, when I lived with someone who was going to law school, I didn't bring up or try to resolve any sensitive or difficult issues during exam times or when a paper needed to be written.

- **ASK YOURSELF:** *"Is openness desirable in this case, at this time?"*

I'll always remember the story a friend told me about the time he chose to tell his family he was gay. He waited until Thanksgiving dinner, when both sides of his large family were assembled around the long dining room table. As the meal was being served he said, "Pass the potatoes, please, and, by the way, I'm gay." The moral of the story is: *Be sure to consider the effects your sharing will have on others and the appropriateness of your timing before you rush into openness.*

- **ASK YOURSELF:** *"Is the person I'm about to open up to trustworthy, supportive, honest, etc.?"*

It's a good idea to determine what you need from the receiver after you share your information. Do you want support? advice? reassurance? A listening ear? Make sure you're talking to someone who can give you what you need.

- **ASK YOURSELF:** *"Will this person understand what I'm going to share or want to understand?"*

One of the issues that's close to my heart is my adoption and the feelings I have about it. Although my friends don't know what it's like to be adopted, some want to understand and therefore encourage me to be open about this aspect of my life. Other friends aren't particularly interested in this, and that's okay; with those people, I share other things about myself.

- **ASK YOURSELF:** *"If I'm going to reveal something about the past, will it be beneficial to my present or future relationship with this person?"*

Too often people share intimate details about their pasts that in no way benefit a present or future relationship. It's a good idea to think about what you hope such sharing can accomplish before you say anything. Remember that sharing details of the past ought to *benefit* your present or future relationship, not take away from it, create conflict, or damage it.

The need for openness, and the resulting intimacy, differs from person to person as well as from time to time in an individual's life and in the progress of a developing relationship. However, the basis for any openness in a relationship begins with honesty in communication.

Think about this . . .

"Oh, the comfort, the inexpressible comfort of feeling safe with a person, having neither to weigh thoughts nor measure words, but pouring them all right out, just as they are, chaff and grain together . . ."
—Dinah Maria Mulock Craik, author of *A Life For a Life*, published in 1859

2. Honesty

Honesty in relationships involves three elements: (1) knowing the truth, which means being aware of the truth; (2) acknowledging the truth, which means admitting it and accepting it; and (3) dealing in the truth, which means verbalizing it.

Healthy honesty begins when you take a realistic look

at yourself and assess who you are and what you want in your relationships (see Chapter Two). For example, you may truly know that you're not ready for a committed, long-term relationship right now. If you ignore this fact and try to be in such a relationship, then you're being dishonest both with yourself and your partner. Likewise, if you know your partner isn't an outgoing, energetic person, expecting that he'll act differently is ignoring the basic truth about his personality.

The first two parts of the definition of honesty focus on knowing and acknowledging the qualities of the people involved in relationships and the characteristics of these relationships. *The goal for developing healthy honesty in these two areas is to accept one another's good and bad qualities and to recognize sensitive areas and items of importance to the people involved in the relationship.*

The third part of the definition involves honesty through verbalization. In Chapter Five, healthy communication is explored in detail. In this section, the focus is on two areas: communication to develop intimacy and communication to work through confrontation and conflict.

Communication to Develop Intimacy

Poor communication is cited as a problem for *90 percent* of married couples who seek counseling. Much of the basis for this statistic results from the inability or difficulty to work through conflicts in a relationship. But some of the reason has to do with the fact that people in relationships often fail to use communication to build bridges to one another, to become closer, to process *good feelings,* and to become more intimate.

Here are some ways communication can be used to develop intimacy with another:

- *Make time to talk.*
  Set a time period of at least 15 minutes to talk with one another about whatever's on your minds. Schedule this time when you won't be interrupted and when you don't have the pressure of other commitments.

- *Give equal time to one another.*
  Break the scheduled time into equal segments so each person has the opportunity to listen and to respond.

- *Refrain from unnecessary interruptions.*
  Promise that you won't interrupt each other, except for necessary clarification.

- *Agree to limit any defensiveness.*
  Make it clear from the start that the point of talking isn't to attack one another, but simply to share what's on your minds.

- *Repeat what you've heard to make sure that it's what's been said.*
  Summarize your conversation with a statement like, *"If I heard you correctly, this is what you said . . ."*

The goal of using communication to develop intimacy is to share your thoughts and feelings with others so you can learn more about each other.

Communication to Work Through Confrontation and Conflict

Common areas of conflict in relationships include confrontation, money, family matters, household tasks, careers, and sex. In order to develop honesty in relationships, all of these sensitive areas—and any others—need to be discussed before they damage the relationship through anger, built-up resentments, and verbal or physical fighting.

Confrontation happens when one person suddenly or unexpectedly states an opposing or conflicting point of view to another person. A confrontation can be minor, such as an error of fact—"No, we're not going on vacation the third. We're leaving on the fourth." It can be more significant, such as a confrontation created by stress or expectations: "I thought you were going to the bank today to withdraw our vacation money. We need that tomorrow." Or a confrontation can be major, such as one caused by intentional or unintentional hurt—"I don't appreciate your making negative comments about me in front of your friends."

Conflict, on the other hand, is the result of a confrontation (cause). A conflict can be handled in unhealthy ways—by argument, refusal to talk, blame, criticism, verbal or emotional abuse, violence, etc.—or in healthy ways.

The goal of communicating to work through conflict in relationships is to use positive, specific methods to process the conflict. These methods include:

- *Giving specific examples of dissatisfaction without attacking a person's character.*
  For example, say, *"I'm really upset that we haven't spent much time together'* rather than *"You've been selfish lately, doing whatever it is you want to do and focusing only on yourself."*

- *Not bringing up someone's vulnerabilities or calling each other names.*
  The last thing in the world I want to hear, if I've just

told someone I'm feeling insecure, is: *"Oh great! Not your adoption issues again!"*

- *Not making assumptions about another person's feelings or thoughts.*
  Ask others how they're feeling, don't *tell* them.

- *Not complaining just to complain, but to bring about positive change.*
  If you don't have a solution or some suggestions for resolving your conflict, no amount of griping will bring about change.

- *Not asking questions when you want to make a statement.*
  For example, rather than ask: *"Do you think we ought to go on vacation?"* say what you really want to say—*"I don't think we can afford to go away now."*

- *Using "I" messages instead of "you" messages.*
  Saying: *"I don't like it when you leave a mess"* is better than *"You're a slob."*

- *Focusing on one thing at a time.*
  If other issues enter the conversation you can say, *"I'm getting confused. I'd like to talk about ____ first and be clear about that before we talk about ____."*

- *Calling for a time out (for at least five minutes, but not more than 24 hours) if either one of you is too angry to process the conflict effectively.*

- *Changing the circumstances in which you argue.*
  You may find a consistent time or situation that triggers conflict; for example, dinner time during the work week. (See Chapter Three—"All About Stress," page 74) Make a rule not to process sensitive issues or argue during that time.

- *Not interrupting.*
  Count to three during a pause in communication or sip water to stifle the desire to break in.
- *ASK YOURSELF: "Is what I'm about to say true?"*
  Sometimes asking such a question can eliminate name-calling, criticism, or anger and can help to build positive, healthy communication.

Think about this . . .

"If you try to study yourself according to another, you will always remain a secondhand human being."
—Philosopher J. Krishnamurti

---

3. Individuality

Individuality means having a sense of self. This sense of self is composed of things that give you personal definition—likes and dislikes, needs and wants, goals and desires, skills and abilities, limits and boundaries. Without a sense of self, you may not develop individuality in a relationship; instead, you may depend on another person to provide you with a sense of who you are or to give your life meaning and purpose.

You don't have to know everything about yourself in order to be healthy or to be in healthy relationships. All you need is the *desire* to get to know who you are, how you feel, and what you want and need. Working on your self-esteem (see Chapter Two) is one way to get in touch with yourself.

Another way is to balance your time alone with the time you spend with others. Alone time gives your mind and emotions the space in which to relax, to let go of tensions and irritations from daily relationship interactions (coworkers, family, friends, intimate partners), to gain new perspective by temporarily distancing from the old, and to rejuvenate—to recharge inner batteries through the limiting of outside stimuli.

Time alone is essential to both people in a relationship. Often this time needs to be scheduled; it also needs to be encouraged, supported, and respected as an essential strengthening component for a relationship.

You might want to structure your days to allow for *a minimum of 15 minutes of alone time every day.* Use this time to go for a walk, take a drive through the country, listen to soothing music, meditate, rent a favorite movie to watch on the VCR, lie in a hot bath, read a book, and so on. The purpose of alone time is to eliminate interactions and outside distractions so you can be with you.

Another method that can increase your sense of individuality with others is to develop separate friends and interests outside your relationships. Too often those involved in intimate relationships look to their partners to satisfy all their needs, whether or not they share common interests. It can be difficult for these people to join groups, classes, clubs, or professional organizations without their partners. They may feel obligated to drag their partners into every friendship. They may criticize one another for time spent apart when this time involves other people or interests. Or they may experience feelings of anxiety, jealousy, or fear whenever interests outside the relationship are discussed or pursued.

But healthy relationships are made of two individuals,

brought together by one or more commonalities, who make a commitment to maintain a variety of friendships and outside interests for the purpose of achieving personal satisfaction, new experiences, and positive growth.

The time spent apart pursuing individual interests, as is the case with alone time, needs to be discussed and scheduled. It also needs to be balanced with the time spent together in the relationship.

The goal of developing individuality in relationships is to help you place a focus on **you**, *for you to do what you need and want to do, not to the detriment of building strong relationships, but to help you become a happier person, with or without others.*

Once the people in a relationship can accept one another for who they are as individuals, nurturing each other can be easier.

Think about this . . .

When pop star Cliff Richard visited a Bihari refugee camp in Bangladesh, he didn't want to touch anyone because they were covered in sores and scabs. But while posing with a small child for a photographer, someone accidentally stood on the child's finger. He screamed. *". . . as a reflex,"* explains Richard, *"I grabbed him, forgetting his dirt and his sores. I remember that warm little body clinging to me and the crying instantly stopped. In that moment, I knew I had much to learn about . . . loving, but that at least I'd started."*

—from *Which One's Cliff?*,
Hodder & Stoughton

4. Nurturing

Nurturing in a healthy relationship means taking care of yourself and giving care to another. The taking and giving need to be kept in balance to ensure that each person maintains a sense of self yet can give time and attention to the other.

In order to nurture another, you first need to learn how to nurture yourself. Nurturing yourself is almost like creating a beautiful flower garden. In order for each delicate flower to be bright and everlasting, you must provide it with the proper nutrition, water, and care. That involves time, commitment, and patience.

You're just as delicate and your needs are just as important. To nurture yourself, you need to learn how to take care of these needs—to give them the proper care and support—and not to expect that others will always be able to do so.

Sometimes this involves a certain amount of positive self-parenting. For example, when you're feeling down, depressed, or under the weather, you can ask yourself: *"What would a loving mother do for her child if the child felt this way?"* Then you can do for yourself what you imagine this loving mother would do.

Sometimes nurturing yourself means giving yourself the things you'd like others to give you—flowers, a box of candy, jewelry, a luxury item, etc. I remember how one of my students used to complain about never receiving any mail other than bills and circulars. So I suggested that she buy a bunch of greeting cards with sentiments she liked and mail them to herself. Now, once a week, she receives a piece of mail she really likes!

Nurturing yourself also means sharing your successes

with others to gain recognition, support, and praise. How many times have you spoken to a friend or family member about the wonderful things you have, what you've achieved, or what makes you happy? Most people find it easier to share information about what they don't have, what they didn't get, what's hopeless to them, or the things that cause them pain.

When you achieve a success of some kind, let other people know how good it makes you feel. Don't belittle it *("Anyone could have done what I did")* or reject it *("It really doesn't mean that much")*. Herald it as something wonderful—announce it to the world! Communicate to others how much it means to you.

Once you begin to nurture yourself, it can become easier for others to know how to nurture you. Recognize your needs and verbalize them to others so they learn what you want and need. Nurturing another means accepting that their needs are important and giving these needs care and attention when it's possible and appropriate.

The goal of developing healthy nurturing in a relationship is to understand how to first nurture yourself, how to nurture another, then how to nurture each other.

As I mentioned earlier, the key to healthy nurturing with others is to achieve a balance that recognizes, accepts, and gives to the needs of both people in a relationship. Sometimes, however, the scales of giving or receiving may be tipped in one direction for a certain amount of time. For example, for eight months during a past intimate relationship, my partner's mother was dying of cancer. During this time period, it was important to our relationship that my partner's needs were given more attention and support, due to the circumstances.

But, over time, the nurturing scales ought to gradually tip back in the other direction, to eventually achieve a balance of giving and receiving so one person isn't placed in the permanent role of care-giver, while the other person becomes a care-taker.

Think about this . . .

Leo Buscaglia advises " . . . *always go into a relationship saying, 'I'm going to make this work, I'm going to find out what it's all about and work at it every single day. I'm going to make it more rich and more exciting and more wonderful. I'm going to bring things to it and take things from it. And I will never take it for granted.'* "

---

5. Knowledge

The final component of healthy relationships encompasses everything you know about trust, honesty, individuality, and nurturing, and which you then apply to your relationships.

Knowledge allows you to make mature decisions regarding your relationships by considering the healthiness of each of these areas. This information is based on realities, not fantasies; facts, not hopes; individuality, not dependency; limitations, not lack of boundaries; change and growth, not stagnation.

Knowledge allows you to answer many important questions about each of your relationships: *Is it healthy?*

Can it grow? Is the other person trustworthy? Honest? An individual? Capable of nurturing? Am I accepted for who I am in the relationship? Are my needs respected? Are we growing together? Are we making healthy changes for ourselves and the relationship?

To help you gain knowledge about your current relationships, you may find it helpful to use the charts on the following pages to assess the role each of the four qualities plays in them. Think about how each quality is exhibited by you and the other person (or people) involved in your relationship(s) and how it affects the overall health of the relationship. If you like, you can write your thoughts in the spaces provided. Use the chart on page 132 as a model.

MY KNOWLEDGE OF MY RELATIONSHIPS

Relationship with *Sam*

TRUST *I trust his fidelity. I trust his love. I don't trust his ability to emotionally support me. As for me, I don't trust my fidelity, but I know I can emotionally support Sam.*

HONESTY *I am not always honest with my emotions, needs, wants, finances, and intentions. I don't believe Sam is honest with his feelings. I think He tells me what I want to hear.*

INDIVIDUALITY *We do all things together. I make feeble attempts at independence, but I fear if I grow individually I may grow away from Sam and end up alone.*

NURTURING *I'm very nurturing when it comes to Sam's needs. I feel he makes sincere efforts to be attentive to my needs. He cares for me when I'm tired, ill, unhappy, etc.*

MY KNOWLEDGE ABOUT THIS RELATIONSHIP
I think I possess a lot of the necessary knowledge for a healthy relationship but don't apply it.

MY KNOWLEDGE OF MY RELATIONSHIPS

Relationship #1:   with _____

TRUST _____
_____
_____
_____
_____

HONESTY _____
_____
_____
_____
_____

INDIVIDUALITY _____
_____
_____
_____
_____

NURTURING _____
_____
_____
_____
_____

MY KNOWLEDGE ABOUT THIS RELATIONSHIP
_____
_____
_____
_____
_____

MY KNOWLEDGE OF MY RELATIONSHIPS

Relationship #2: with _____

TRUST _____
_____
_____
_____
_____

HONESTY _____
_____
_____
_____
_____

INDIVIDUALITY _____
_____
_____
_____
_____

NURTURING _____
_____
_____
_____
_____

MY KNOWLEDGE ABOUT THIS RELATIONSHIP
_____
_____
_____
_____
_____

MY KNOWLEDGE OF MY RELATIONSHIPS

Relationship #3: with _____

TRUST _____
_____
_____
_____
_____

HONESTY _____
_____
_____
_____
_____

INDIVIDUALITY _____
_____
_____
_____
_____

NURTURING _____
_____
_____
_____
_____

MY KNOWLEDGE ABOUT THIS RELATIONSHIP
_____
_____
_____
_____
_____

The goal of developing knowledge in each of your relationships involves using what you know about trust, honesty, individuality, and nurturing to make changes or strengthen positive elements to work towards creating happier, healthier relationships.

Think about this . . .

"When you love someone," writes Anne Morrow Lindbergh, *"you do not love them all the time, in exactly the same way, from moment to moment. It is an impossibility . . . And yet this is exactly what most of us demand. We leap at the flow of the tide and resist in terror its ebb . . . Security in a relationship lies in living in the present relationship and accepting it as it is now."*

RELATIONSHIP LIFEGOALS

Now write your RELATIONSHIP LIFEGOALS. You may find the suggested Goal Starters helpful in creating your goals. Be sure your goals are specific to your relationship needs.

YOUR IMMEDIATE RELATIONSHIP GOAL(S): to be achieved within the next few minutes to the next few hours.

GOAL STARTER: *I'm going to decide what I want to do tonight—spend time alone, spend time apart, or spend time with my intimate partner.*

_____

_____

_____

YOUR SHORT-TERM RELATIONSHIP GOAL(S): to be achieved within one week to one month.

GOAL STARTER: *I want to work on the conflicts in my relationship with my boss by saying what I mean, rather than telling him/her what she/he wants to hear. I'll assess the effects of my efforts at the end of each week.*

_____

_____

_____

YOUR MID-TERM RELATIONSHIP GOAL(S): to be achieved within one month to one year.

GOAL STARTER: *I want to develop my individuality in my relationship with my family by enrolling in a course at the local college three nights a week. I'll ask my spouse for help preparing dinner and taking care of the kids on those nights and recommend that he pursue something that interests him on non-conflicting nights.*

_____

_____

_____

YOUR LONG-TERM RELATIONSHIP GOAL(S): to be achieved within two to four years.

GOAL STARTER: *I'm going to work on developing trust and openness in my relationships by sharing myself with others.*

_____

_____

_____

YOUR RELATIONSHIP TARGET GOAL(S): indefinite.

GOAL STARTER: *I'm going to make a commitment to work on my relationship with _____ to see if this is the person with whom I'd like to spend the rest of my life.*

_____

_____

_____

READ ON

Beyond Codependency And Getting Better All the Time, by Melodie Beattie, Hazelden Educational Materials, 1989.

Codependent No More, by Melodie Beattie, Hazelden Educational Materials, 1989.

Love, by Leo Buscaglia, Fawcett, 1972.

Love Is Letting Go of Fear, by Gerald G. Jampolsky, M.D., Bantam Books, 1970.

Making Changes: How Adult Children Can Have Healthier, Happier Relationships, by Amy E. Dean, Hazelden Educational Materials, 1987.

*Books and pamphlets can be ordered from Hazelden by calling 1-800-328-9000.

*"Signs of Healthy Love" (pamphlet), by Brenda Schaeffer, Hazelden Educational Materials, 1986.

Smart Love, by Jody Hayes, Jeremy P. Tarcher, Inc., 1989.

*"What Is Normal? Family Relationships" (pamphlet), by Amy E. Dean, Hazelden Educational Materials, 1988.

Why Love Isn't Enough, by Sol Gordon, Ph.D., Bob Adams, Inc., 1989.

Women Who Love Too Much, by Robin Norwood, Pocket Books, 1985.

5 □ COMMUNICATION

How You Verbalize Who You Are and What You Want

Communication is defined as the external (verbal) expression of who you are. (Communication also encompasses nonverbal expression through body language, touching, gestures, facial aspects that indicate feeling, and so on, but this chapter focuses solely on verbal expression.)

You verbally express yourself in many ways: through explaining, conveying facts, expressing an opinion, or simply talking. How you express yourself, how this expression is received by others, and how you feel about your ability to communicate are key factors in how healthy your communication skills are.

Unhealthy verbal communication comes in two forms: *aggressive communication* and *passive communication*. Verbalizing, to aggressive communicators, is much like playing a tennis game where the two people are constantly batting balls (words) back and forth with the goal of scoring points (winning). Aggressive communicators often talk loudly, speak quickly, and interrupt frequently. Sometimes they may threaten physical violence to get their points across.

Examples of statements or responses made by aggressive communicators in conversations include: *"The discussion is over." "I'm not asking you, I'm telling you." "How could you be so stupid?" "F____ you!"* . . . and so on.

Passive communicators, on the other hand, are often shy, soft-spoken, easily intimidated, and unclear with the messages they convey. They usually have great difficulty volunteering information about what they want or need. In addition, it's often hard for them to share their thoughts and feelings openly and honestly.

A passive communicator might use responses such as: *"Anything you say," "It doesn't matter to me," "I'm fine," "You're right," "I don't know,"* . . . and so on.

A *healthy communicator* recognizes that *both* the speaker and the listener have certain rights. A healthy communicator allows a speaker to complete whatever he or she has to say, without interruption (except for clarification), by giving the speaker complete attention. Then the listener responds to the speaker by giving feedback, asking questions for elaboration, and saying whatever he or she needs to say, without interruption and with the listener's complete attention.

Healthy communication is complete and fulfilling, both to the speaker and to the listener.

Here's an example of a dialogue between two healthy communicators:

She: *I see that we can't easily express feelings with each other.*

He: *Really? I hadn't thought much about it.*

She: *I have. I think we could really do a lot better with sharing our feelings.*

He: *Okay. Where do we start?*

She: *Well, I think we need to be more open with each other. I'd like you to tell me how you feel about the things that are important to you in your life—your job, your friends, and your family, for example.*

He: *I'm open to doing that. Will you tell me how you feel about the things in your life, too?*

She: *By all means. I want you to know how I feel. I think it's important for us.*

He: *I do, too. I'm glad you brought this up.*

She: *Thanks for listening.*

YOUR MOTIVATORS

Each of the following statements reflects some of the thoughts, feelings, and behaviors of a person who has healthy communication skills. Do these statements accurately reflect your current level of communication?

- *"I'm rarely misunderstood when I communicate with others."*

- *"I know what I'm going to say before I say it."*

- *"I give and receive feedback during my conversations."*

- *"I process conflicts within a 24-hour period."*

- *"I make time to discuss issues that affect my relationships."*

- *"I always speak with a clear, crisp, controlled tone of voice."*

- *"I use communication to improve my levels of intimacy with friends, family, and an intimate partner."*

- *"I listen and give full attention to what others say."*
- *"I ask questions when I'm confused or unclear."*
- *"I'm not afraid to talk to people."*
- *"I don't interrupt others who are speaking."*
- *"I respond to what's said, not to what I think I hear."*
- *"I'm not afraid to say 'I don't know' or 'I'm not sure.'"*
- *"I communicate my feelings openly and honestly."*
- *"I state my opinions, even if they differ from others."*
- *"I speak up whenever I feel uncomfortable or annoyed."*
- *"I feel confident and comfortable when I speak with others."*
- *"I communicate my boundaries clearly to others."*

People with healthy communication skills are usually relaxed and confident. They're equally comfortable with inner dialogue as well as in discussions with others.

Healthy communicators are empathetic to their own needs as well as to the needs of others. They know the importance of respecting and verbalizing these needs, so they don't criticize, put down, analyze, or try to control the thoughts and feelings expressed by others. In addition, they won't give advice unless asked nor preach to others about the rights and wrongs of their words or behaviors.

Healthy communicators look upon conflict as times of growth and resolution. They're willing to negotiate and compromise to achieve harmony with others. They're ready to let go of anger easily and effectively and will not shut off communication in order to manipulate or punish another.

Healthy communicators verbalize who they are and

what they need or want assertively, not aggressively. They stand up for themselves and express their true feelings, but in ways that are considerate of the needs of others.

Think about this . . .

> "To express unafraid and unashamed what one really thinks and feels is one of the greatest consolations of life."
>
> —Psychologist and author Theodor Reik

Communication is a process that happens on two levels: *the level of experience* and *the level of expression.* The level of experience is particularly significant; it's based on what you learned in your childhood about communication and the behavior habits you formed as a result.

Most children learn their communication skills from their parents or siblings. For example, you may have been taught that it's "bad" to talk about a feeling. You may have learned that shouting is the only way to get a point across. You may have been told that intimate thoughts are best left unspoken or that the appropriate way to work through a problem is to keep it to yourself.

Whatever your parents or siblings taught you about communication when you were a child forms the basis for your level of experience in this area today.

Think about this . . .

Criticizing a person's actions or attitudes, labeling a person by name calling, and analyzing the reasons behind a person's actions by playing amateur psychotherapist restrict healthy communication.

Criticizing: *"You're making a mountain out of molehill," "Any fool could have done what you did,"* etc.

Labeling: *"What a dope!," "You're such a jerk,"* etc.

Analyzing: *"You know you're doing that just to start an argument," "I bet you feel pretty damn cocky right now,"* etc.

To improve your communication, remove these restrictors from your conversations. When others use them with you, point out how limiting such expressions can be (for example, say, *"How would you like me to respond to that?"*) and suggest methods of improving their communication with you (for example, say, *"I don't appreciate being called a name. I'd like to deal with the issue at hand, not personalities"*).

Think about how your parents communicated with you and your siblings and with each other while you were growing up. How did they express their feelings? How did they work through conflicts? Were family problems discussed openly and honestly? Were there aggressive, passive, and/or non-communicative styles in your childhood home?

Aggressive communication involves arguing, verbal and physical fighting, accusing, threatening, and abusing people in a way that shows little regard for their feelings. If you were raised in a dysfunctional home, then you probably understand what aggressive communication is all about. You know first-hand that the "positive" element of aggressive communication—if there can be a positive element to such behavior—is that few people will stand up to the person who communicates in this way. Aggressive people usually get their way. But aggressive communication distances people from each other; thus, aggressive communication doesn't help relationships.

Passive communication is exhibited by people who allow themselves to be pushed around by others, usually aggressive communicators. Passive people do and say what others want them to do and say. Passive people are often well liked because they do everything others want them to. But, because passive people don't often get to do what they want, they're often angry, frustrated, and disappointed with themselves and their inability to stand up for themselves and to communicate what they need or want.

A perfect example of aggressive and passive styles of communication came from one of my student's descriptions of a typical dialogue heard in her dysfunctional (physically and verbally abusive) childhood home:

Dad (yelling at Mom): *"You dumb bitch! Get my dinner on the table now! Clean up this dump! You're a lazy, good-for-nothing broad!"*
Mom: *"I'm sorry, I'm sorry. I'll get your dinner right now. Please don't scream at me. Please don't hurt me."*
Me (thinking in my room): *"That asshole! Why does she put up with him! Maybe I should go downstairs and help her. Maybe that will shut him up."*

Non-communication is another unhealthy approach. It can be based in anger (for example, using defiant silence as a weapon or as a form of punishment) or it can be designed to "protect" someone (for example, refusing to relate bad news, criticism, innermost secrets, and so on, rather than hurt or cause unhappiness to another). Non-communication prevents people from relating to one another on a talking/ feeling level, thereby creating relationships based upon tension, resentment, and built-up frustration.

In summary, aggressive people communicate by attack, passive people communicate by being victims, and non-communicators withdraw from communication. These methods of communicating are unhealthy.

Think about this . . .

Diverting a person's attention away from a problem he or she would like to discuss, over-reassuring someone to prevent them from expressing emotions, and trying to be a problem-solver restrict healthy communication.

Diverting: *"Let's talk about something else," "Let me tell you what happened to me,"* etc.

Over-reassuring: *"Don't worry. Every cloud has a silver lining," "It'll be okay,"* etc.

Problem-solving: *"If I were you, I'd . . . ," "What's the big deal?" "Here's what you should do . . . ,"* etc.

To improve your communication, remove these restrictors from your conversations. When others use them with you, point out how limiting such expressions can be (for example, say: *"If you were upset and needed to talk, would you like it if I changed the subject?"*) and suggest methods of improving their communication with you (for example, say: *"I'm not sure things will be okay, and that's why I need you to listen to how I feel"*).

The level of experience you bring into your communication in adulthood influences how well you communicate not only with yourself, but also with others, which has a great impact on the relationships you form (see Chapter Four).

Your level of experience also indicates how confident

and comfortable you are verbalizing your thoughts, feelings, wants, and needs. You may find verbal expression difficult if you're influenced by beliefs such as the following. Do you share in any of these beliefs?

- *"I don't know if I can be honest."*
- *"If I say something, I think the other person will be angry."*
- *"I don't think I say things 'right.'"*
- *"I'm afraid I'll be judged if I open my mouth."*
- *"What I say always comes out wrong."*
- *"I'm very critical and negative."*
- *"I'm anxious about not being clear."*
- *"I feel people will say I'm too pushy if I say what I want."*
- *"I find it hard to get what's in my head out my mouth."*
- *"I feel insecure talking to people."*
- *"I'm not sure I'll be understood."*
- *"It's better if I hold things in."*
- *"I gear my communication to what I think others want to hear."*
- *"I can't express my anger well."*
- *"It's hard for me to say how I really feel."*
- *"I won't talk about issues that may cause a confrontation or emotional discussion."*
- *"I feel uncomfortable talking to an authority figure (boss, parent, husband, etc.)."*

Such beliefs, or attitudes, can "talk you out of" wanting to talk things out!

Think about this . . .

Commanding another person to do what you want them to do, threatening someone with negative consequences, and telling another person what he or she *should* do restricts healthy communication.

Commanding: *"Do it because I said so . . . ,"* *"I don't care what you want; this is what I want . . . ,"* etc.

Threatening: *"You might as well forget about sex tonight if you do that," "You're going to be in big trouble now,"* etc.

Telling: *"You should say you're sorry," "You should have never become involved with her,"* etc.

To improve your communication, remove these restrictors from your conversations. When others use them with you, point out how limiting such expressions can be (for example, say: *"How would you feel if I said that to you?"*) and suggest methods of improving their communication with you (for example, say: *"Telling me what I shouldn't have done is helpful, but what I need is for you to listen to me"*).

COMMUNICATION LIFEGOALS help you rise above many of these negative communication beliefs by strengthening weak communication skills and promoting assertive behaviors in your actions and interactions. COMMUNICATION LIFEGOALS can help you work through such common conflicts as:

- *"Why can't I say what I really mean?"*
- *"How can I identify and communicate my needs to my-self and others?"*
- *"Why do my discussions with my intimate partner always end up as arguments?"*
- *"How do I learn to set my own boundaries and limits?"*
- *"How can I stand up for myself?"*

When you make COMMUNICATION LIFEGOALS, you're giving yourself the opportunity to improve *your level of understanding about your own needs and also the level of openness and honesty in your interactions with others.*

In addition, by learning how to verbalize what you want, need, or mean in a healthy way, the messages you verbalize will be clearer. As a result, you may find yourself getting what you want in life—from your relationships, from your career, from your family, and from yourself.

YOUR MISSION

To begin setting COMMUNICATION LIFEGOALS, first determine a few missions for your goals and outline them on the COMMUNICATION MISSIONS CHART. Your missions are based on:

1. Your particular communication problem areas (Who Are you Now?);

2. What you need or want from your goals (What Do You Want to Achieve?); and

3. The type of person you'd like to become or the life you'd like to have once you achieve your goals (Who Will You Be? or How Will You Be?).

COMMUNICATION MISSIONS CHART

Who Are You Now?
Example: *I am a person who has difficulty expressing my feelings when I am angry.*
1. _____
_____
2. _____
_____

What Do You Want to Achieve?
Example: *I want to be able to communicate, even in the heat of a moment, without losing my temper or using physical violence.*
1. _____
_____
2. _____
_____

Who Will You Be? or How Will You Be?
Example: *I see a person who's calm and collected under pressure, who's clear and succinct, and who will not be drawn into argumentative, abusive behavior.*
1. _____
_____
2. _____
_____

Your Mission
Example: *I want to create a goal to learn more about how to work through my anger so I may express myself during emotional times.*
1. _____
_____
2. _____
_____

YOUR FOCUS

All About Communication

Although communication is the external expression of who you are, communication always begins as an *internal process* first.

*This means that you need to know what you want **before** you can tell others.* You do this by "listening" to and understanding your feelings.

Internal communication is *always* based on feelings (external communication doesn't always deal on a feeling level). But feelings do not move from your heart directly to your mouth. Rather, feelings are often *filtered* first through your mind before they're even acknowledged to the self or verbalized to others.

The word *filtered* is critical due to the way in which this process can affect the open and honest expression of your feelings, both to yourself and to others. Mind filters operate in the following ways: they can minimize how you feel ("You're not *really* angry, are you?"), encourage you to look at your feelings in a negative way ("You need not feel that way."), or urge you to suppress your feelings ("Don't feel that anger!").

When mind filtering happens, you don't get the true picture of how you really feel. This hampers your ability to maintain open and honest channels of communication between your heart and your mind and ultimately affects the information that you relate verbally.

Why does mind filtering occur? Predominantly, mind filtering is a result of the conditioning you had while you were growing up. You may have been taught that expressing certain feelings wasn't appropriate; for example, that it wasn't okay to feel anger. So, in adulthood, your mind continues to tell you not to feel angry—it filters your anger when you're really angry.

Filtering also occurs when your mind passes judgment on how appropriate it is to express a feeling in a particular situation or at a particular time. For example, several years ago I was going through an emotional upheaval at the same time that I started a new job. For about a month, I felt tears of sadness well up almost every hour. But my mind filters urged me to "shut off" my sadness because crying on the job wasn't appropriate.

Another basis for mind filters are the fears, real or imagined, of what you think will happen if you express your feelings. It's this type of filtering, for example, that prevents people from verbalizing three important words, *"I love you."* The fears of exposure, vulnerability, abandonment, and rejection often dictate suppressing the expression of this and other wonderful feelings.

Finally, mind filters can come from trying to anticipate what will happen in the future as a result of expressing a feeling in the present. For example, wanting to shout at a loved one could be altered by mind filtering that cautions, "Don't get angry now. You're just starting to get along with each other, and showing your anger will only make things worse."

But whatever the reasons, mind filtering profoundly changes the original feeling and can sometimes prevent you from knowing exactly how you feel. What follows is an example of how the mind can filter a simple feeling, and thereby alter it.

REAL FEELING: *"I am sad."*
MIND FILTERS:

- Past Habits—*"Don't cry. Big girls/boys don't cry."*

- Present Appropriateness—*"I mustn't cry in public, even if the theater is dark."*

- Fears—*"People will think I'm stupid if I start crying during this scene."*

- The Future—*"I want my date to like me. I'd better not cry, or I may jeopardize whether or not we see each other again."*

MIND-FILTERED FEELING: *"It's stupid to feel this way. There's no reason for me to be sad."*

Such negative mind filters can distort your feelings and make it difficult to acknowledge and express your feelings openly and honestly, both to yourself and to others.

Communicating with others means telling them, through words, who you are and how you feel. It's important, therefore, that your level of internal communication deals with your feelings without the mind filters. Don't think, *"I mustn't feel this feeling," "It's not appropriate to feel this feeling,"* or *"The consequences of this feeling won't be great."* Instead, examine the feelings you experience in a situation or conflict by asking yourself these questions:

- *"What do I think?"*

- *"How do I feel?"*

- *"Is this a present-day feeling (now) or a reaction to something from the past (then)?"*

- *"What do I want to do?"*
- *"Do I want to say anything?"*

These questions help you to *accept* the feeling that you have; to *think* about whether it's occurring as a result of something happening in the moment or in relationship to something from your past; to *decide* what you need, want, wish, or desire at the present moment in regards to the feeling, and to *make a choice* whether or not to verbalize this feeling.

Accept, think, decide, and *make a choice* are the healthy components of internal communication. The goal in developing healthy communication with yourself is to be aware of what you're feeling, where the feeling is coming from, what you need as a result of the feeling, and whether this feeling is something you choose to share.

To return to the "I am sad" feeling, here's how you can process this feeling without the mind filters, with the five questions in mind:

FEELING: "I am sad."

ASK YOURSELF: "What do I think?"
"I think this is a particularly moving scene in the movie."

"How do I feel?"
"I feel like I want to cry."

"Is this a present-day feeling (now) or a reaction to something from the past (then)?"
"This scene is about a mother-daughter relationship and death, and I remember how I felt when I watched my mother die."

"What do I want to do?"
"I want to hold my date's hand for comfort."

"Do I want to say anything?"
"I think eventually I'd like to be able to tell someone the impact my mothers' death had upon my life. For now, I can tell my date that I'm moved by the scene."

Another way to develop internal communication without mind filtering is to keep a journal. A journal allows you to voice your thoughts and feelings in a safe space, one in which your mind is not allowed free rein to distort or deny the existence of how you feel.

To continue the "I am sad," example, here's how a sample journal page might appear:

"Wow! I saw Terms of Endearment *last night with Bob, and I almost became teary. The scene in the hospital between Debra Winger and Shirley MacLaine was so moving. It reminded me of seeing my mother in her hospital bed before she died and wanting to say the 'right thing' to her. I've never talked to anyone about my mother's death. I guess that's why I felt so sad when I saw the scene right in front of me."*

Removing mind filters helps you become clearer with yourself. This, in turn, can help you communicate more clearly with others.

As I mentioned earlier, communication is a process that happens on two levels: *the level of experience* and *the level of expression*. The *level of expression* is the external process of communication; this means verbalizing who you are and what you feel to one or more people.

There are two styles of verbal communication:

1. winning; and

2. improving the quality of your relationship with another.

The *winning style* involves one person who monopolizes the verbalizing process or who interrupts constantly to prove his or her points.

The *quality style* involves two people working together to achieve a balance of give-and-take during conversations so there's an appropriate amount of giving and receiving feedback. The quality style also involves recognition and understanding of three forms of communication—listening, silence, and talking—which were identified and described by Joseph Libo in 1959.

Think about this . . .

> *"There are people who, instead of listening to what is being said to them, are already listening to what they are going to say themselves."*
> —author and dramatist Albert Guinon

Listening

There are two levels of listening involved in communication. The unhealthy level includes the listening in which you're formulating your answer, interrupting, or daydreaming. Most people are guilty of this level of listening because English is spoken at a rate of 200 words per minute, yet can be listened to at a rate of 500 words per minute. So, to fill up the "dead air" time, it becomes tempting to stop listening and to pay more attention to yourself and your own thoughts.

Healthy listening, called *active listening*, is where you give your full attention to the speaker. An active listener listens for the feelings expressed by another by paying attention to body language (the way someone communicates feelings and the attitudes assumed during speaking) and the tone of a speaker's voice. The active listener then verbally acknowledges the feelings observed and heard in a way that encourages the person to say more about them.

The messages an active listener gives to the speaker are: *"I see you . . . I hear you . . . I know you . . . and you're okay."*

Active listening brings the speaker and the listener closer together; it allows each time to listen to one another and thus gain a greater mutual understanding.

The goal of active listening is to completely share the feelings first rather than to talk about outcomes. This means that it's far more important to get your feelings across rather than to give advice.

Think about this . . .

"The talkative listen to no one, for they are ever speaking. And the first evil that attends those who know not how to be silent is that they hear nothing."
—Plutarch

Silence

There are two levels of silence in communication. There's the silence in which you withdraw from talking and take time to interpret the messages being sent to you. There's also the silence in which you take an official "time out" to refresh and rejuvenate your outlook on the situation being discussed. Silence is vitally important to communication because it allows you time to become secure in your emotions, to interpret the messages being sent to you, and to process how you plan on communicating your feelings to the other person.

The goal of developing healthy silence in communication is to become more comfortable with moments of silence. If this is difficult for you, you might want to practice counting to ten before you respond during a dialogue.

Talking

There are five levels of talking that determine the depth of intimacy and sharing that can be achieved during a conversation.

1. Cliché Conversation, which is very light. For example: *"Hi. How are you? Nice weather, huh?"* Cliché conversations are usually filled with cliché responses, which keep the depth of intimate dialoguing to a minimum.

2. Reporting Conversation, which states facts about people, situations, and things. For example, *"Did you hear about . . . ?"* This kind of conversation is a bit more personal than cliché conversation, but the exchange of information is kept on the who-what-when-where-why-how reporting level.

    3. Idea/Judgment Conversation, which relates your ideas and/or judgments about people, situations, and things to others. For example: *"I like . . ."* or *"I don't like . . .".* This kind of conversation has the potential to move into more intimate dialoguing.

    4. Feelings Conversation, which reports how you feel about something. For example, *"I was really moved by what you said. That meant a lot to me."* Such conversation opens the doors to more in-depth communication.

    5. Peak Conversation, which involves being emotionally open and honest with another person and accepting, in return, that person's feelings and responses.

Feelings and peak conversations, combined with active listening and healthy silence, can be used to develop assertive and intimate conversations with people. Yet too few conversations incorporate these qualities. Most people seek out cliché, reporting, and idea/judgment conversations because they're easier to handle and less threatening. These forms of talking are okay to use to "touch base" with people who aren't close to you.

    But when you need to assert yourself with others or when you need to develop openness, honesty, and trust, feelings and peak conversations are recommended.

    The goal to developing healthy communication is to effectively use four levels of talking in a five-step process that focuses on how you feel and what you need so you can verbalize your feelings and needs clearly, openly, and honestly.

    Here's how.

Five-Step Healthy Communication Model

This five-step communication model combines reporting conversation, idea/judgment conversation, and feelings conversation into a healthy step-by-step process for developing peak conversational exchange. If the person with whom you're speaking is also familiar with this process, you may find you're both able to work through situations and conflicts much easier.

1. **State what you see or hear** by using an "I see . . ." or "I hear . . ." statement.
Example: *"I see that you are angry I'm late for dinner."*

2. **Give your interpretation of what you see or hear** by using an "I think . . ." or "I believe . . ." statement.
Example: *"I think you have a right to be angry."*

3. **Tell how you feel** by using an "I feel . . ." statement.
Example: *"I feel mad at myself when I do this to you."*

4. **Relay what you want or need in the form of a request for something** by using an "I want . . ." or "I need . . ." statement.
Example: *"I want you to allow me an extra half hour to arrive on time for dinner."*

5. **Tell what you'll do in return if your want or need is met** by using an "I will . . ." statement.
Example: *"I will call you if I'm going to be late again."*

This step-by-step model incorporates the primary principle of healthy communication, *which is that you're responsible for everything you say, including all the seen or un-*

foreseen consequences. The model is helpful because it serves to minimize conflicts, yet maximizes the exchange of personal feelings, wants, needs, and desires.

A student in my class used this peak conversation model to help her resolve a two-year conflict in a relationship with her intimate partner. Their conflict involved an alarm clock and a set of expectations that both of them had, but neither could effectively communicate.

Here's the letter Jamie wrote to her boyfriend Carl, in which she used the five-step communication model (emphasis added).

Dear Carl:

__I see__ that you've set the alarm clock for 4 a.m. again. I don't think it would be so bad, but I hear it going off every morning while you sleep through it. Then I have to climb over you, fumble for the snooze button, and get comfortable only to have to do it all over again in ten minutes. __I think__ you're trying to drive me nuts when you ask me to help you get up the night before, but give me grief when I try to do what you ask the next morning.

__I feel__ very angry, put out, and taken advantage of by the time you "come to" at 5:30.

__I need__ your cooperation. I would like to reach a compromise.

__I will__ still help you get up in the morning, and you can still have the alarm on your side of the bed. All I want is to set the clock for 5:00 or even 4:45 instead of 4:00.

What do you think?

Love,
Jamie

Jamie and Carl were able to resolve their issue. They agreed to set the alarm for 4:45 a.m., and since that decision has been made, they've had conflict-free mornings. Carl commented that Jamie's letter communicated her feelings to him very clearly. Although he knew all along that the alarm clock was a sore spot for them, he had never been able to resolve the issue in the past. "But I can't argue with Jamie's letter," he said. "She was clear. It was up to me to respond and to address her suggested compromise."

Unhealthy communication perpetuates uncomfortable situations and allows negative behaviors to flourish. Healthy communication resolves conflicts and gives positive behaviors a chance to grow.

YOUR COMMUNICATION LIFEGOALS

Now write down your COMMUNICATION LIFE-GOALS. You may find the suggested Goal Starters helpful in creating your goals. Be sure your goals are specific to your communication needs.

YOUR IMMEDIATE COMMUNICATION GOAL(S): to be achieved within the next few minutes to the next few hours.
GOAL STARTER: *I'm going to express my anger when I feel it.*

_____

_____

_____

YOUR SHORT-TERM COMMUNICATION

GOAL(S): to be achieved within one week to one month.

GOAL STARTER: *I'm going to be more aware of my mind filters. I'm starting a journal today and will write in it for 15 minutes every night for the next two weeks.*

YOUR MID-TERM COMMUNICATION

GOAL(S): to be achieved within one month to one year.

GOAL STARTER: *I'm going to use the five-step model for communication for the next two months with my intimate partner.*

YOUR LONG-TERM COMMUNICATION

GOAL(S): to be achieved within two to four years.

GOAL STARTER: *I want to work on overcoming my shyness, so I'll make efforts to attend at least five social affairs a year with coworkers and/or friends over the next few years.*

YOUR COMMUNICATION TARGET GOAL(S):

indefinite.

GOAL STARTER: *I want to eliminate the bickering in my marriage so we can achieve peace in our communication. To that end, I'd like to process things as they occur and try* *to resolve them as quickly as possible. If necessary, I'll suggest couples counseling to work on communication.*

READ ON

Effective Listening: Hearing What People Say and Making It Work for You, by Keven J. Murphy, Bantam Books, 1988.

How to Start a Conversation and Make Friends, by Don Gabor, Simon & Schuster, Inc., 1983.

People Skills, by Dr. Robert Bolton, Simon & Schuster, Inc., 1979.

Your Perfect Right, by Robert E. Alberti and Michael Emmons, Impact Press, 1987.

When I Say No, I Feel Guilty, by Manuel J. Smith, The Dial Press, 1987.

6 □ CAREER/LIFEWORK

How to Achieve Challenge, Satisfaction, and Fulfillment

 A career is made up of particular tasks or jobs in a field that you're dedicated to or participate in on a full-time or part-time basis and for which you receive financial reimbursement. Lifework differs from a career in that it doesn't necessarily include payment as a benefit. Examples of lifework are volunteering, internships, pursuing a college or graduate school degree, being a homemaker, serving on the board of a charitable organization, and so on.

The important qualities to look for in either a career or lifework are *a level of challenge, a sense of personal satisfaction, and an element of fulfillment.*

Challenge encompasses the learning—both about the career/lifework you've chosen to pursue and about yourself—that gives you a sense of change, growth, and freshness in what you're doing. Challenge can be provided by education, training, new experiences, greater responsibilities, a growing personal awareness about what you want and need, and so on. It's up to you to determine what *level* of challenge you desire to keep your interest high and your motivation strong.

Some people need a high level of challenge on a daily basis. One nurse may enjoy emergency room work because of the great demands it places upon her. Another nurse may savor the routine of a scheduled 7 a.m. to 3 p.m. shift on a floor. Yet both can be challenged in ways that make them feel satisfied.

I recall how it felt to not be challenged at a job. When I was working as an Associate Editor at a small publishing company, there was never enough new product to keep me busy. Each day, I adhered to the schedules of the work I needed to do, but I found I completed my work long before the day was over. For a short time, I tried slowing my work pace. However, I soon left the job, not because I didn't like what I was doing, but because it simply didn't provide me with the challenge I needed.

Personal satisfaction comes from the sense of purpose or meaning a career or lifework gives you. For some, this satisfaction comes from helping others. For others, this comes from achieving personal goals. Still others receive satisfaction from the recognition or rewards they achieve as a result of their career/lifework. And there are those who feel satisfied when they're allowed to use their skills or creativity. While challenge is the motivator (the cause) in a career or lifework, satisfaction is the result (the effect) of the effort exerted in the challenge.

Finally, career/lifework needs to provide an element of fulfillment in your life. Fulfillment is the measure of how your career or lifework contributes in positive ways to your *entire* life—your personal relationships (family, friends, intimate partner), your relaxation time (play, hobbies, meditation, stress management), and your self-development (health and fitness, learning, positive growth and healing). Career/lifework that's fulfilling complements and is in balance with the other parts of your life; it doesn't dominate them or detract from them.

Achieving challenge, satisfaction, and fulfillment in your career/lifework is the purpose for setting career/lifework LIFEGOALS.

Think about this . . .

> *"There's no work too hard,"* says writer Eddie Robinson, *"if it gets you what you need or where you want to go."*

YOUR MOTIVATORS

Each of the following statements reflects some of the thoughts, feelings, and behaviors of a person who receives challenge, satisfaction, and fulfillment from career/lifework. Do these statements accurately reflect your experiences in your career/lifework?

- *"I feel energized to start my day."*
- *"I enjoy what I do."*
- *"What I do is valuable to me and has meaning."*
- *"I have a positive attitude in my career/lifework."*
- *"I have many skills and use them effectively."*
- *"I'm good at what I do."*
- *"I know my options and make choices that are right for me."*

- *"I communicate my needs to others."*
- *"I'm not manipulated or controlled by others."*
- *"I try to learn something new every day."*
- *"I handle the pressures and stresses of my career/lifework in positive ways."*
- *"I don't let my career/lifework interfere with my relationships."*
- *"I keep my career/lifework in balance with my other interests."*
- *"I don't take on more than I can handle."*
- *"I ask for help when I need it."*
- *"My career/lifework is rewarding and fulfilling."*
- *"I don't do my career/lifework perfectly, but I do it as well as I can."*

People who achieve challenge, satisfaction, and fulfillment from their career/lifework have a healthy attitude toward their work. They know how to balance work time with time for rest and relaxation, for family and relationships, and for self-development. They have realistic expectations from their work and don't expect a career or lifework to provide them with everything they need or want in life. They keep their work in perspective and refrain from thinking of themselves, in their professional roles or their work, as the be-all or end-all to everything. They let go of their need to be perfect in their work and strive to do the best they can.

When their skills and abilities need to be strengthened, they're ready to do so through education or retraining. They're often clear with their definition of work success and do what they can to become successful.

And, finally, they know that in order to achieve challenge, satisfaction, and fulfillment in their work, they need to be willing to make any changes necessary to help them reach those goals.

Today I don't have to look far to find a role model who has achieved challenge, satisfaction, and fulfillment in her work. In working for myself—writing the books I want to and choosing the freelance clients who offer me exciting projects—I truly believe I have found my niche. I am challenged every day, am totally satisfied with what I do, and have achieved total fulfillment from my work.

But I haven't always felt that way in my work, and now I know the reasons why. Let me share them with you.

Too often people expect their career/lifework to give their lives meaning—to bring them all the happiness they think they deserve or that has been so elusive, to provide them with all the "answers" (no matter what the questions are!), to give them a sense of self-esteem or personal worth, and so on.

But people can spend their whole lives chasing rainbows and mythical pots of gold with this way of thinking—that a career/ lifework is somehow going to "bring it all together," and make one rich in the process!

And all too often, people expect that they'll easily find the "right" career/lifework that will give their lives profound meaning. So, they focus on a career or specialized field and decide that that's what will keep them happy and fulfilled for the rest of their working days. And if or when this doesn't occur, they blame the company they're in, the people they work for, their family—anything or anybody—to keep from reassessing their choices about work or making changes.

But as businessman C. W. Metcalf once advised, *"Take your work seriously but yourself lightly."* Don't you think it might be a bit unrealisitic to expect that one small interest, in the wide array of interests that exist in the world, will keep someone happy day in, day out, for the next 30, 40, or 50 years? While I love to write and have written many books, I don't think, "This is what I'd like to do for the rest of my life." *Anything* can lose its challenge or appeal over time. While there's a strong possibility I'll write for the rest of my working life, I may vary the types of writing I do, limit the amount of time I spend writing, or pursue other work if and when my writing doesn't challenge me, bring me satisfaction, or help me achieve a sense of fulfillment.

People often don't realize the wide range of career/lifework options they have available to them at any given moment, whether they're working or not. If they're not satisfied and fulfilled from their work, they might not be aware of the options and choices available for them.

What are the career/lifework options available? There is job hunting while employed and job hunting while unemployed. There is staying in a career of one's choice, but doing the same thing in a different location, within a different department, or with a different group of people. There is staying in the same career or line of work, but moving to a new position in the field, at the same location or with a new group. There's choosing a new career or lifework, on a part-time or full-time basis. There is choosing to work for oneself by working for others on a contract or freelance basis, by working a few part-time jobs, or by choosing one interest and working solely on that. There is volunteer work or internships. And there is going back to school, which involves even more choices: deciding on a major, choosing a school, and so on.

"People aren't looking at their job as a lifelong develop-ment, as a way to grow," comments Sharon Danann, research director at a Cleveland-based group called *9 to 5, National Association of Working Women.* A friend of mine told me about a conversation he had recently that validated Ms. Danann's statement.

He was telling a young man about his talented daugh-ter, who was going to live in New York City after she graduated from college to try to make her way in the tough world of the theater.

"Why's she going to do that?" the young man asked. "Why doesn't she just star in a movie or something? Go out to Hollywood? Then she'll be discovered and won't have to worry about anything."

Hmmm. We're living in a society today where we don't have to wait for anything, where we don't have to put a tremendous amount of energy into a whole lot of things. Cooking dinner? Zap a full-course meal in the microwave in less than two minutes. Are your clothes dirty? Pop them in the washer. Need a new dress but have no money? Hop in the car and head to the nearest retail store, where anything can be paid for with a piece of plas-tic. Miss your family? Fly across the world in a matter of hours to see them.

Want a career or lifework? According to the young man I mentioned earlier, star in a movie if you want to act. Pen a bestseller if you want to be a writer. Become the president of a large corporation if you want to be a business success. Invent a cure for cancer if you want to be a famous doctor.

I remember graduating from college and thinking, "I'll land a job on a big city newspaper as a reporter and write stories that'll win Pulitzer Prizes." Instead, I landed a job as a temporary secretary in a publishing company, where I had to work hard every day to prove that my talents ranged far beyond my ability to type 60 words a minute.

Careers and lifework require lifelong development. They also require adaptability because *they* develop, change, and grow over time. If you can develop, change, and grow along with them, then you may find great happiness in your work.

In 1985, I was laid off from my job as a Senior Copywriter at a large game manufacturing firm. I really liked that job. I was working in a creative, fun environment. I was given the opportunity to work with game designers and to pursue a lifelong interest in art. I was allowed to dabble in advertising and marketing copywriting. I took graduate-level writing courses and began a mystery novel I'd always wanted to write. In short, I felt challenged, satisfied, and fulfilled at this job.

For six months after I left, I looked for other jobs in writing, but couldn't find anything I felt would give me the same sense of freedom and creative challenge as I had had with the game manufacturer. I spent a great deal of time complaining. I felt stress and pressure. It became difficult for me to sleep at night.

Then, one sleepless night, I picked up a daily meditation book and read it. "This writing is wonderful and calms me down," I thought, "but it's focused on what I can do in the morning to make my day go better. My day's already gone."

As I flipped through the book, I remembered how the game designers had worked. They were each given charters, or definitions, for various projects they needed to provide for the sales year; for example, an action board game, based on a license, for boys 7 to 12 years old; an indoor/outdoor toy for family play, etc. Then they'd brainstorm—make lists—of ideas that would satisfy their particular charters.

That's what I did that night. I brainstormed the format and design of a night-time meditation book. I thought about the market for the book and the publisher.

The next morning, I wrote a marketing proposal for the book, composed some sample pages, then mailed my idea to a few publishers.

A few months later, I signed the contract on NIGHT LIGHT, a book of evening meditations. To work on the book yet keep the money flow steady, I found a job as a part-time English tutor at a junior high school. I was hired to coach a high school speech team. I landed a few freelance assignments from my former employer.

That was in 1986. As you read this book now, I'm the author of four books and a lecturer in the field of adult children from dysfunctional families. I now write self-help books for the mass market, as well as fiction.

The moral of my story is: In order to achieve happiness from my career, *I* had to change, develop, and grow because my work had changed, developed, and grown in an unexpected direction. Whether I would have made the same choices or ended up in the same career as I am today is debatable, but not important at this point.

The key is to always be aware of the options and choices you have in your career/lifework, no matter what twists or turns occur in that chosen path, and to be ready to make choices or changes when necessary.

Think about this . . .

"We work to become, not to acquire."
—Journalist Elbert Hubbard

The best career/lifework you can have teaches you more about yourself, about those you love, and about the world around you. To leave yourself open to the possibilities that your work can bring you, as well as to leave your work open to the changes you can bring it means your work can be more personally rewarding and, therefore, more challenging, satisfying, and fulfilling.

Making CAREER/LIFEWORK LIFEGOALS can help you identify what kind of worker you are and what skills and abilities you have, which can ultimately help you make work decisions that are compatible with you and your capabilities. CAREER/LIFEWORK LIFEGOALS can also help you work through some of the self-defeating behaviors you may presently experience in your work so you can have a more positive, motivated outlook now and in the future. Finally, CAREER/LIFEWORK LIFEGOALS assist you in looking at your work as a series of step-by-step goals, rather than as decisions cast in stone, which are often difficult to change.

CAREER/LIFEWORK LIFEGOALS can help you work through such common conflicts as:

- *"Why am I such a perfectionist?"*
- *"How can I become a healthy worker and not a workaholic?"*
- *"How do I learn how to define success?"*
- *"How can I achieve a more healthy balance of work time with personal time?"*

When you make CAREER/LIFEWORK LIFEGOALS, you're giving yourself the opportunity to achieve the greatest challenge, satisfaction, and fulfillment from work activities that demand your time, attention, and energy.

YOUR MISSION

To begin setting CAREER/LIFEWORK LIFEGOALS, first determine the missions for your goals and outline them on the CAREER/ LIFEWORK MISSIONS CHART. Your missions are based on:

1. Your particular career/lifework problem areas (Who Are You Now?);

2. What you need or want from your goals (What Do You Want to Achieve?); and

3. The type of person you'd like to become or the life you'd like to have once you achieve your goals (Who Will You Be? or How Will You Be?).

CAREER/LIFEWORK MISSIONS CHART

Who Are You Now?
Example: *I am a person who wants to work for myself.*

1. _____

_____

2. _____

_____

What Do You Want to Achieve?
Example: *I need to feel fulfilled from my own decision-making, and not the decisions made for me by others.*

1. _____

_____

2. _____

_____

Who Will You Be? or How Will You Be?
Example: *I see a person who is making good money, working out of the home in a mail-order catalog business.*

1. _____

_____

2. _____

_____

Your Mission
Example: *I want to create a goal that involves enrolling in marketing courses that focus on mail-order sales and starting my own business.*

1. _____

_____

2. _____

_____

YOUR FOCUS

Achieving Challenge, Satisfaction, and Fulfillment from Your Career/Lifework

The purpose of creating LIFEGOALS in the area of career/lifework is to achieve challenge, satisfaction, and fulfillment from what you're doing now and what you'd like to do in the future. This section will not address the mechanics of career counseling. Instead, it will focus on *ten tools* you can use to help set goals to assist you in achieving challenge, satisfaction, and fulfillment in any career you choose or lifework decision you make. (NOTE: For in-depth guidelines on career counseling, I highly recommend Richard N. Bolles' *What Color Is Your Parachute?* listed in the "Read On" section, and books that deal with career/lifework areas of interest to you.)

Tool #1: Who Am I?

Sometimes who you are at work and who you are outside of work can make you feel like a Jeykll and Hyde personality. You may wonder why the patient self your friends and family knows disappears the moment you walk into your office building. You may be confused about why you're a firm and decisive decision-maker outside work, but can vacillate for hours over the color of the cover of your company's annual report.

Who you are at work—and how happy you are with this "person"—can play a big role in how challenged, satisfied, and fulfilled you feel from your work.

If you like who you are at work or who your work helps you become—both at work and outside work—then chances are your job provides you with positive energy that helps you feel challenged, satisfied, and fulfilled. But if you don't like who you are at work or if you feel that you're one person at home and another person on the job, your work may leave you confused, incomplete, or frustrated.

On the chart below, or on a separate sheet of paper, you may wish to list words that describe who you are outside work and who you are at work. I filled in the chart with words that describe how I felt on one of my jobs.

WHO I AM OUTSIDE WORK	WHO I AM INSIDE WORK
Example: *trusted, patient, confident, satisfied*	Example: *scattered, low confidence, confused, frustrated*
_____	_____
_____	_____
_____	_____
_____	_____
_____	_____
_____	_____
_____	_____
_____	_____
_____	_____

After you think about who you are at work and who you are outside work, take note of any similarities or differences. Are you the same person in and out of work, or do you become someone different? These differences or similarities are important; they can give you clues to help you determine the level of challenge, satisfaction, and fulfillment you experience from your work.

For example, I felt very comfortable with myself outside work but was a scattered, confused, frustrated person at work. This indicated to me that my work was more stressful than challenging, more frustrating than satisfying, and more physically and emotionally damaging than fulfilling.

If you have similar feelings from your career/lifework, you might consider setting goals that help you make changes in yourself so you can better handle your work, such as including stress reduction techniques or meditation in your daily routine, for instance (see Chapter Three). You may want to set a goal that includes asking for assistance on projects to ease stress caused by overwork. You may set a goal that includes exploring work opportunities in a different department in the same company or in a different company. Or you might believe that burnout is the root of your stress and may set a goal to take time off or to explore other work options.

I remember reading an article about former basketball coaches of the Boston Celtics and the changes that occurred in the men's personalities once they stepped into their roles as pro basketball coaches. Bob Cousy reported having nightmares and being incapable of eating a meal in one sitting. Jimmy Rodgers began losing his hair. Tommy Heinsohn's temper flared at the most minor of incidents.

On the other hand, Hubie Brown, the volatile former coach of the New York Knicks, said: *"You have to prevent yourself from getting an ulcer, an alcohol problem, getting into drugs, getting under psychiatric care or getting a divorce. For me, it included time for game preparation, physical activity, proper diet and a rest period."*

To me, Hubie Brown's attitude emphasizes that taking a look at who you are inside and outside work can help you identify *strengths* you're building at work that you might not ordinarily exhibit in your personal life. For example, you may be the one chosen to give major presentations to your company's stockholders because you handle yourself with grace, poise, professionalism, and confidence.

Yet outside work, you may find talking to a friend difficult. In such a case, you might wish to set goals that help you replicate your positive work behaviors in your interactions with family and friends. For example, if you can decide the color of your company's annual report in ten seconds but can't make up your mind between hamburgers and pizza for dinner, you can set goals to help you become as decisive a person at home as you are on the job.

The key to setting goals in the area of personal identification is to determine your positive and beneficial qualities and to exhibit these qualities both at work and outside work.

Tool #2: Skills Indentification

Sometimes people don't feel challenged, satisfied, or fulfilled in their work because they think that their skills (talents, abilities, training, background, etc.) aren't being utilized to the fullest. Other times people are unhappy at work or drift from job to job because they don't know what skills they have or what they're good at.

"Skills," explains Richard Bolles, author of *What Color Is Your Parachute?*, *"are your God-given talents, gifts, aptitudes, or whatever. The name does not matter. They are the essence of what you have to offer to the world, within the world of work."*

What are your skills?

Setting goals in the area of skills identification relies upon your ability to first know all the skills you have—both work-related and nonwork-related—which skills you'd like to utilize in a work environment, and what skills (existing or to be explored) you'd like to develop (at work or outside work).

On page 186 are two *Skills Identification Triangles*—mine, which is completed, and yours, which you may wish to complete. Note the number and diversity of My Skills in the bottom of my triangle. It's important for you to record *everything* you're good at, whether or not you'd consider it to be something you'd like to bring to a work environment. People often don't realize how many things they're good at, nor do they always consider that some of their skills, which may spring from hobbies or other spare-time activities, are skills they can bring to a work environment—and can derive great satisfaction from doing so.

My job with the game manufacturing firm, for instance, provided me with challenge, satisfaction, and fulfillment because my skills included game-playing abilities and the invention of new games. Notice the skills I've recorded in the Work Skills section of the triangle. These are the ones I bring to work as well as the ones I'd like to see utilized in a work environment. After you think about or record your work skills, determine how effectively these skills are currently being used. What you discover can help you focus on changes you'd like to make in your present position (to include more skills, for example) or in finding a position elsewhere that will utilize your skills in more challenging, satisfying, and fulfilling ways.

Finally, in the *Skills To Be Developed* section of the triangle, think about the skills you'd like to have the opportunity to develop either at your current job or outside of work. Think of these skills as dreams, desires, or wishes—areas you might not be good at, but which you'd like the opportunity to explore. You can then set goals to help you explore how to include these areas in your present work. In my case, I was able to begin my mystery novel through the company's policy of tuition reimbursement for work-related classes (writing). And, had I not been laid off, I would have been able to take a drawing class and get a chance to develop that skill.

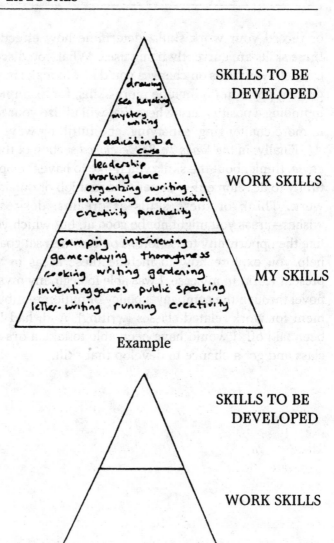

SKILLS TO BE DEVELOPED

drawing
sea kayaking
mystery writing
dedication to a cause

WORK SKILLS

leadership
working alone
organizing writing
interviewing communication
creativity punctuality

MY SKILLS

Camping interviewing
game-playing thoroughness
cooking writing gardening
inventing games public speaking
letter-writing running creativity

Example

SKILLS TO BE DEVELOPED

WORK SKILLS

MY SKILLS

Knowing your skills and combining and developing them with work-related activities can strengthen the skills and give you a sense of satisfaction and fulfillment.

Tool #3: The Life Pie

The *Life Pie* is a quick exercise designed to give you an idea of how effectively you're presently balancing your work time with time you set aside for play (relaxation, pursuing hobbies, vacationing, etc.), self-development (health and fitness, education, personal growth, etc.), and relationships (with family, friends, intimate partner, etc.).

Based on the results of this exercise, *you can set goals to help you bring a more equal balance in your life so work-related activities aren't dominating, controlling, or playing havoc with the other parts of your life.* As Hubie Brown commented, *"It's okay to get a divorce, but not if it's a result of your job."*

To begin this exercise, keep track of how many hours per day, *for a total of ten **average** days (not vacation days, holidays, or sick time),* you spend on the four "pieces" of the "pie": work, play, self-development, relationships. Record your times on the chart on page 188 or on a separate sheet of paper. Then, in the "pie" below the chart, draw lines that determine the size of the pieces in each area of your life. The results of your pie division can help you determine the goals you may need to set to help you achieve greater balance in activities throughout your life.

YOUR LIFE PIE

	Work	Play	Self-Development	Relationships
Day 1				
Day 2				
Day 3				
Day 4				
Day 5				
Day 6				
Day 7				
Day 8				
Day 9				
Day 10				
TOTAL:				

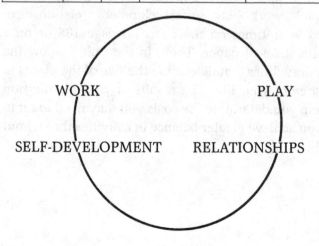

WORK   PLAY

SELF-DEVELOPMENT   RELATIONSHIPS

Tool #4: Power

Often people think of power as control of or over others, such as that exhibited by a manager, supervisor, teacher, or other authority figure. Or, power is considered to be a material measurement of worth, such as that symbolized by an enormous salary, a new BMW, or an elegant home.

If you think of power in such terms—the amount of control you have over others or what you can earn with that control—then your work-related goals may be based on the struggle to get rather than to grow. It may be very difficult, then, to find challenge, satisfaction, and fulfillment from a career or lifework because you're continually on the lookout to achieve ever-greater amounts of power.

I define power as the end result of excelling at something or distinguishing yourself in some capacity. It's through the excellence or achievement that you exhibit your power, which is your capacity to be seen in a different light or to receive recognition and reward as a result of your achievement.

If you do well during a corporate presentation, for example, then you've achieved power because you've allowed yourself to be recognized as capable of handling other presentations.

This definition of power allows you to set goals focused on personal achievement, with the emphasis on achieving for personal growth rather than for personal gain.

Tool #5: Logical Perspective

Whenever I think of keeping work-related circumstances in a logical perspective, I'm reminded of the commercial for one of the popular next-day delivery companies. The scene: an employee receives a call from a hysterical client, who screams that if he doesn't get the product he ordered the next day, he's out of business. What happens? Since the employee uses another overnight delivery service, not the advertiser's, the product arrives days late, when the client is already out of business.

I remember working under the pressure of similar dire warnings at former jobs. More often than not, artwork came in late, and designers caught the flu, and printers lost mechanicals, and proofreaders fell behind, and authors didn't meet manuscript due dates. People I talk to about their work tell me similar tales of botched schedules—delayed airline flights and undelivered construction materials and computer snafus and a multitude of other hassles.

To the best of my knowledge, no *major* catastrophes have resulted from these human or nonhuman delays, either in the companies I've worked for or in the companies people I know work for. Time still marches on, the sun sets and rises, and the world spins 'round and 'round. Life, as well as work, goes on.

The key to keeping your work in a logical perspective is to recognize what's important and what isn't, and then to focus on what you can humanly do about what's important and let go of what you can't do.

Tool #6: A Healthy Attitude

A healthy attitude, as it relates to work, involves balancing work-related activities in a way that benefits your life as a whole. Those who don't have a healthy attitude are workaholics who live, eat, and breathe their jobs. They're the people who take a vacation, but who bring work with them and call the office every day. They're the people who say they socialize outside the office, but who interact on the golf course with potential clients and business partners. They're the people who consider telephone calls from children during the workday an intrusion and have virtually no energy to devote to family members when they arrive home late at night.

The keys to developing a healthy work attitude are moderation and flexibility. Moderation allows you to keep the components of your life in balance (as in the Life Pie) so each area receives the time, attention, and energy it deserves.

Flexibility is the component that unlocks the ability to adapt and change—to go with the flow—even if the flow takes you away from work for a certain amount of time.

Think about this . . .

"Time is like a river made up of events that happen, and a violent stream; for as soon as a thing has appeared it is carried away, and another comes in its place; and this will be carried away too."
—Marcus Aurelius

Tool #7: Time

Wouldn't it be wonderful if some of the excitement, anticipation, and growth you experienced in the first job you liked held true for the rest of your life? But time has a way of changing circumstances and feelings. What you want or need from work when you're in your twenties is a lot different from what you want and need from work when you're in your thirties, forties, fifties, or sixties.

People often go through five major cycles in their work experiences, which can challenge their growth in their jobs, question their level of satisfaction with their work, and sometimes deny them a sense of true fulfillment:

The Twenties

This is the time when people question what they want to do with their lives and search for an occupation. "I've always thought I wanted to work in the medical field," one of my 23-year-old friends recently told me. "I've thought about becoming an x-ray technician, studying sports medicine, and enrolling in nursing school. I guess I just can't make up my mind."

The Thirties

This is the time when people reassess the work choices they made when they were in their twenties. They may continue in their careers, get married and focus on raising a family, relocate, change careers, and/or return to school. When one of my students was in her mid-thirties, she left a lucrative marketing job in a large corporation to enter law school, with the ultimate goal of practicing public interest law.

The Forties

This is the time when people notice how their work relates to or affects their relationships, marriage, living situations, etc. This is also the time when people feel they have their "last shot" at satisfying their work dreams. Sometimes women who have been mothers and homemakers since their mid-twenties return to school or enter the work force. Some people may make radical career changes; for example, a teacher may leave the teaching profession to open a retail business.

One of my co-workers, when he turned 48, purchased several acres of land in a remote location in Maine. He decided the time was right to start making his dreams come true: to live in Maine and illustrate children's books. For the past few years he has commuted a few hours every weekday to his old job; nights and weekends he spends building his home. His goal, once the home is completed, is to take early retirement and begin working for himself.

The Fifties

This is the time when people often question whether they've accomplished what they set out to and ponder the worth of their work achievements. This is often a period of great introspection that can sometimes result in personal satisfaction or depression and disappointment.

"I realize now that I have no place to go in the company," one of my friends recently told me. "All I can hope to achieve is lateral movement, but I had wanted to become a manager by the time I was 55. Now I don't know what to do. I guess I have to rethink my career goals."

The Sixties

This is the time of endings, as people look ahead to retirement. Personal energy level is often low, and anxiety about the unknown leads many to focus outside their work to possible relocation, hobbies, finances, etc.

One couple I know sent for information on the Peace Corps when they each turned 60. They wanted to remain active once they retired and were concerned that they might not be able to achieve challenge, satisfaction, and fulfillment without a focus.

If you can adapt well to the changes that take place over time, then you'll have a much better chance of setting and achieving realistic and satisfying work goals.

Tool #8: Expectations

The two most important questions you can ask about a career or lifework are:

1. **What do I want?**
2. **Can I get it?**

What you may want may be very different from what you can really get, which can create great conflict and lead to unrealistic work expectations.

For example, you may want your supervisor to be your mentor—someone on whom you can rely and learn from and who can help you better your position in a company. But can your supervisor deliver what you want? An interesting article in *Behavioral Sciences Newsletter* reported that almost half the managers who participated in an employee relations IQ test didn't understand that people repeat behavior that's rewarded; more than 60 percent didn't think it was right to brag about their subordinates' accomplishments; and almost 80 percent didn't understand that observations made in performance reviews should be specific rather than general.

Thus, it's important that you keep your work expectations realistic. Don't set your sights so high or make your wants so unreachable that you set yourself up for disappointment. You'll be better able to achieve challenge, satisfaction, and fulfillment when your expectations can be met.

Tool #9: Success

Success means different things to different people. To some, it's a corner office and gold-embossed business cards. To others, it's an extensive client list and the feeling of being in demand. Still others believe success is measured in financial terms. And there are those who believe that success is helping others rather than helping themselves.

Think about this . . .

Louis L'Amour, the prolific writer of Western novels, once commented, *"People often expect success suddenly, and that's the worst thing that could happen. The years of struggle and commitment and learning are part of the process of building a storehouse of know-how that will help you excel at your trade."*

In order to achieve work success, it's important to define what success means to you. Is it money? prestige? achievement? Or is it doing what you want to do for as long as you'd like to do it? As Liz Smith has simply stated, *"Success, to me, is loving your work."*

Once you determine your view of success, you can set goals that help you work towards achieving it.

Tool #10: The Five "Cs" of CAREER/LIFEWORK LIFEGOAL Setting

Finally, it's important to keep in mind "the five Cs" to help you with your career/lifework goal-setting:

1. Change

You need to be willing to make changes, both in your work and within yourself, to ultimately make your work challenging, satisfying, and fulfilling. As Dolores Hope, wife of comedian Bob Hope, advises, *"Your life is going to be as interesting as you make it. Keep active. Keep working. Keep trying. And don't be afraid of change."*

2. Creativity

Keep in mind that there's *always* another way of looking at things. Approach your work changes from different angles. Visualize new ideas and use the creative power necessary to implement your vision of the way things can be. *"Could 'Hamlet' have been written by a committee or the 'Mona Lisa' painted by a club?"* asks A. Whitney Griswold in the book *In the University Tradition*. *"Creative ideas do not spring from groups. They spring from individuals."*

3. Communication

Ask for assistance from others, gather the information that can help you, and verbalize what you want or need clearly and assertively.

4. Confidence

Believe in yourself!

5. Commitment

Stick with your goals. See them through, then revise them or change them as necessary.

YOUR CAREER/LIFEWORK LIFEGOALS

Now write your CAREER/LIFEWORK LIFEGOALS. You may find the suggested Goal Starters helpful in creating your goals. Be sure your goals are specific to your career/lifework needs.

YOUR IMMEDIATE CAREER/LIFEWORK

GOAL(S): to be achieved within the next few minutes to the next few hours.

GOAL STARTER: *I'm going to look into what training programs are available that can help me acquire the skills necessary to be promoted in my career.*

_____

_____

_____

YOUR SHORT-TERM CAREER/LIFEWORK

GOAL(S): to be achieved within one week to one month.

GOAL STARTER: *For the next month, I'm going to work on perfectionism on the job and will try to let go of some of the control I have by asking for help with large projects.*

_____

_____

_____

YOUR MID-TERM CAREER/LIFEWORK

GOAL(S): to be achieved within one month to one year.

GOAL STARTER: *For the next six months, I'm going to keep a work log in which I'll track the amount of time I spend at work or working on job-related materials, the time I spend with my family, and the time I spend doing the things I like to do.*

_____

_____

_____

YOUR LONG-TERM CAREER/LIFEWORK

GOAL(S): to be achieved within two to four years.

GOAL STARTER: *I'd like to start a family and assess how I feel about giving up my career and taking on lifework as a mother and homemaker six months after having my second child.*

YOUR CAREER/LIFEWORK TARGET GOAL(S): indefinite.

GOAL STARTER: *I want to go back to school for a graduate degree in law and pursue public interest law opportunities in the Southwest.*

READ ON

Business Games: How to Recognize the Players and Deal With Them, by Martin G. Groder, M.D., Boardroom Classics, 1989.

Changing Your Life, by Strephon Kaplan-Williams, MFCC, Journey Press, 1987.

Home Away From Home, by Janet Geringer Woititz, Ed.D., Health Communications, Inc., 1987.

The Relaxation & Stress Reduction Workbook, by Martha Davis, Ph.D; Elizabeth Robbins Eshelman, M.S.W.; Matthew McKay, Ph.D; New Harbinger Publications, 1982.

Self-Renewal, by Dennis T. Jaffe, Ph.D. and Cynthia Scott, Ph.D., M.P.H., Simon & Schuster, Inc., 1989.

The Seasons of a Man's Life, by Daniel J. Levinson, Ph.D., Alfred Knopf, 1987.

The Seasons of a Woman's Life, by Daniel J. Levinson, Ph.D., Alfred Knopf, 1988.

The Three Boxes of Life . . . And How to Get Out of Them, by Richard N. Bolles, Ten Speed Press, 1981.

What Color Is Your Parachute? by Richard Nelson Bolles, Ten Speed Press, updated annually.

Work Addiction, by Bryan E. Robinson, Health Communications, Inc., 1989.

7 □ YOUR PERSONAL WEALTH

How to Manage Your Money to Enrich Your Life

 Wealth is commonly associated with affluence and riches. When people say they want to be wealthy, what they usually mean is that they want to have a lot of money so they can spend it freely without feeling guilty and without going into debt.

*But I think of **your personal wealth** as your ability to manage the money you earn or have—whatever that amount may be—and to plan how to effectively use that money now and in the future so you can achieve a sense of financial security. Financial security* can help enrich your life; when you're financially secure you're free from worries about money, free from excessive debt, and free from the fear of poverty. When you're financially secure, you feel confident that you'll be able to provide for your basic needs today and tomorrow.

To become financially secure, you need to be able to design a financial plan that helps you meet your expenses, save for the future, and spend for your personal enjoyment. *LIFEGOALS for your personal wealth help you work*

with *the money you earn or have and help you take control of your finances so you can get the most from your money.*

Think about this . . .

Money is a good servant but a bad master.
—French proverb

YOUR MOTIVATORS

Each of the following statements reflects some of the thoughts, feelings, and behaviors of people who are financially secure. Do these statements accurately reflect your sentiments about your personal wealth?

- *"There are riches and abundance in my life."*
- *"I'm able to financially support myself (and others who need my support)."*
- *"There's little that I want or need."*
- *"I'm happy, whether or not I have money."*
- *"I'm living within my means."*
- *"My worth can't be measured in terms of money."*
- *"I pay my bills on time."*
- *"I like to give a portion of my money to charitable causes when I can."*
- *"I don't expect others to take care of me financially."*
- *"I can ask for a raise (or for more money from a parent or spouse)."*

- *"I spend my money wisely."*
- *"I always have a little money tucked away 'for a rainy day.'"*
- *"I look for the best value for my money; I don't buy impulsively."*
- *"I know exactly what I earn and what my expenses are."*
- *"I like spending money on myself."*
- *"I can afford to take my dream vacations."*

People who have a high level of personal wealth know exactly how much money they make (earnings, less taxes and other deductions), what their expenses are (daily, weekly, and monthly living expenses as well as outstanding debts), how much money they need to set aside or save in order to achieve their financial goals (for example, the purchase of new car or luxury item, making a down payment on a house, paying college tuition, etc.), and how much "free money" they have available for their immediate enjoyment (movies, dining out, clothing, etc.).

Since I started working for myself in 1986, I've become a good money planner/manager. I never have trouble meeting my expenses, even though I must deduct federal and state taxes from my earnings, pay for my own health insurance, and contribute to my own retirement plan—without even knowing what my actual earnings are! As a writer, I work on a royalty basis, so every year's sales are different. I receive my biggest royalty check in late September, which means I have to budget for nine months of the *next year* on what I receive in that check. With my earnings, I make mortgage payments every month on a house, I've purchased a late model used foreign car *with cash*, I take short trips every two or three months, and I always have enough money to go out for a night on the town.

Today I feel wealthier than I've ever been in my life, but that's because I now know how to manage the money I make. That has not always been the case.

When I worked for employers, I received a paycheck every week in which taxes were already taken out and my retirement contributions were deducted. My medical insurance was paid for by the company. Each week, I knew exactly how much money I was taking home but, invariably, by the time I received that check, I was on my last dollar. I felt like I was barely staying ahead of the bills that were nipping at my heels. I lived frugally, but it never seemed that I was frugal enough. If I was given a raise, the additional money always seemed to be spent before I got it. Money was an ever-present concern. Although I wasn't living beyond my means, and I was pulling in a good salary, I couldn't figure out where my money went and why it went so fast.

But once I learned how to manage my money and make sound financial plans, I was able to take control of my financial future. To make this dramatic change, the first thing I needed to learn were the money-management characteristics that distinguished a person who has a good sense of his or her personal wealth from a person who does not.

People who are financially secure:

- have some money-management skills, or the ability to make financial plans;
- save a percentage of their income off the top, then live off the rest;

- know exactly what they're worth (everything they make/own);
- know exactly where their money goes (what they owe to whom);
- deposit their checks quickly;
- make specific financial goals (instead of saying, "I want to buy a new car," they say, "I want to buy a new car two years from now, so I'll put aside $50.00 a month to build up a good down payment);
- make serious goals (purchasing a house) as well as fun goals (taking a vacation);
- have money set aside for an emergency (major car repairs, replacement of an appliance, etc.);
- control their use of credit cards and limit their borrowing;
- invest only in what they understand or feel comfortable with or for that which they've received sound professional advice;
- reward themselves with intermittent "treats" (purchasing a luxury item, taking an unexpected trip, etc.).

People who are financially secure work hard at making their money work for them so they can feel confident and secure with their sense of personal wealth. They apply effective money-management skills to create a personal budget and savings plan that works for them. But, more importantly, people who are financially secure maintain a *rational* relationship with money, where they treat money only as a means of exchange and not as the prerequisite for leading a happy and fulfilling life.

Before you can apply money-management skills in

your life, it's important to first take a look at if and how money affects you emotionally. Think about your answer to this question: How do you *feel* about money?

Think about this . . .

> *"Happiness lies not in the mere possession of money; it lies in the joy of achievement, in the thrill of creative effort."*
> —Franklin Delano Roosevelt

Some people spend their lives chasing after money. They forget (or deny) that money is only " . . . clam shells or metal discs or scraps of paper," as described by Napoleon Hill, author of *Think & Grow Rich*. They associate money with control and power and prestige. They believe they would be so much happier if they had more of it. So they equate their sense of personal fulfillment and satisfaction with money; they feel that the more money they have, the better they'll feel about themselves and their lives. To these people, money buys them their sense of self-esteem and determines their happiness.

I remember a conversation I had with my father when I graduated from college and had rented my first apartment; it illustrates this concept of money equals happiness. He called me one night to tell me he wanted to buy me furniture for my place.

"That's a really nice offer, Dad," I responded, "but I think I'd like to pick up things myself, a little bit at a time. I won't be able to afford much right away, but I think that's how I'd like to do this. I need to support my-self on the money I'm making, not on the money you've made."

Then I asked him, "How does it feel, Dad, to have everything you've ever wanted? You can buy anything. You have a beautiful fifteen-room house with lovely fur-niture, a new car, and you take lots of trips. It'll be years before I can have those things. You must feel great!"

He was silent for a moment. Then he replied, "You know, Amy, some of the best memories I have are from the days when I lived in a small apartment furnished with orange crates. I was pretty happy back then. Money doesn't buy happiness. I have a lot today but, well, the days of the orange crates were fun, too."

My Dad's words stayed with me from that night on. And the day I tossed my last orange crate out the door, I knew my life had undergone a major change.

Money can be very emotional. Talking about it often makes people anxious, causes couples to argue, breaks up marriages, creates animosity between friends, and is the source for on-the-job resentment. "People are more will-ing to discuss their sex lives than their salaries," agrees Dr. Edward Hallowell, an instructor in psychology at Har-vard Medical School and author of *What Are You Worth?* "When we do discuss money, we like to surround it with numbers—interest rates and other data—that give it a scientific aura. But we're simply trying to dodge the powerful emotional factors that govern the way we feel."

Instead of dealing rationally with money, most people

let the powerful tidal wave of emotions generated by the search for greater amounts of coins and dollar bills crash upon their thinking process so strongly that money begins to dominate their lives. Some people chase after money as if it were the meaning to life. Napoleon Hill describes this pursuit of money: *"It (money) must be wooed and won by methods not unlike those used by a determined lover . . ."* Some people become greedy and exhibit this greediness in two ways: by trying to accumulate as much money as possible (through stinginess, miserly behaviors, or by hoarding money) or by compulsive spending or over-spending, in which the reward is not the actual purchases themselves but the ability to purchase.

Dr. Hallowell comments on this: *"People are quite willing to put themselves in extremely precarious financial situations to keep up with the Joneses, to have their kids go to private school or to join the right country club . . . Some people owe more on their credit cards than they make in a year!"*

I had never thought much about the concept of greed until I went to a racetrack one Saturday afternoon. As I was standing in line to place a bet, a man behind me said, "You're five dollars short, lady."

"Excuse me?" I replied.

"When you reached into your pocket for your money a few moments ago, a five-dollar bill dropped to the ground."

I looked down, but only saw discarded tickets.

"It's gone," he explained. "A guy saw you drop the money, and he picked it up, quick as a wink, and ran off with it."

"You're kidding!" I exclaimed.

"Nope."

I shook my head. "I don't believe it. I wouldn't have done that. I would've handed the money back."

"That's what *you* might've done, lady. But you're at the track. People here are desperate for money. They'll take it any way they can get it."

Greed is very common today. In many cases, it's the driving force that motivates people to pursue money. But most often, greed is a reaction to fear: fear of poverty, fear of failure, fear of not being good enough, fear of not being accepted, and so on. These fears aren't easy for most people to let go of. Advertising bombards us every day with the messages that in order to be better people, we need to buy more, more, more. The media directs our attention to the lifestyles of the rich and famous—multimillionaires like Donald Trump, superstar athletes like Michael Jordan, and movie actors or actresses who command incredible salaries—and glorifies these lives. And the government continues to reward the richest in our population and take from the poorest.

For some people then, money talks louder than the voice of reason.

Think about this . . .

> "I'll give you an example that shows the main reason I'm uncomfortable with the press," Boston Celtics basketball star Larry Bird said in a rare interview in March 1990. "Last week I was in Miami and a newspaperman asks, 'Larry, how many more years are you going to play?' And I answer facetiously, 'I want to be the first player in the league to make $10 million.'
>
> "It was a joke! The newspaperman knew it was a joke! But next day the headline read that Larry Bird was planning to be the first player in the league to make $10 million! It made me sound greedy."

Sometimes people use money to chase "the blues" away. They make purchases that help them feel better about themselves, even if the feeling is only temporary. The motto that I've mentioned before—"when the going gets tough, the tough go shopping"—is indicative of this need to use money to buy happiness.

Other times people foster and maintain "a relationship" with money—stockpiling it, investing it, moving it around, adding it up—and spend more time focusing on their money and money-related matters than on friends and family. The character who best illustrates this kind of behavior is the infamous Ebenezer Scrooge, who lost his business partner, family, and friends because of his love and lust for money.

Finally, in order to understand the emotional impact money may have upon you today, it's important to examine what kind of messages you received about money as a child. Think about how your parents handled money.

- *Were they overly frugal?*
- *Overspenders?*
- *Always in debt?*
- *Did you grow up rich, poor, middle class?*
- *Did you receive an allowance? If so, how did you earn it?*
- *Did you receive the same amount every week or month, or did you receive money upon demand?*
- *Did you start working before you left your childhood home?*
- *At what age?*
- *If you worked, who controlled your earnings?*
- *Did you contribute any of your money to your household?*
- *Save any of it?*
- *On what did you spend the money you earned or received for an allowance?*

An examination of your money history may help you shed light on the basis for an emotional relationship you may have with money today. Let me give you an example. One of my friends used to live in a sparsely furnished, tiny apartment. She rarely turned the heat on in her apartment, never went out to dinner, and wore clothes that not only had long since gone out of style, but were quite the worse for wear. There was no reason for her to live in that fashion. But rather than spend any of the generous salary she earned, she banked most of it and then sat at home in the cold, with an afghan wrapped around her.

One day we went shopping together. She tried on an inexpensive pair of slacks but refused so vehemently to purchase them that I was quite taken aback.

"What's the problem?" I asked her. "You live like you're a pauper. There's no reason why you can't buy yourself something nice every once in a while."

"Yes, there is!" she snapped back. "I can't spend my money. Not one cent of it!"

"Why?" I asked.

"I grew up in the poorest section of town," she replied, her voice shaking. "There was never enough food. I lived on potato chips and Cokes for meals. My parents never had enough money. They argued constantly, but their worst arguments were about the money they had to spend on us kids. Amy, you grew up with food, clothing, books, movies—anything you wanted. I grew up with nothing."

"But today you're a successful engineer," I reminded her. "You can buy anything you want on your salary."

She nodded. "In reality, I know I can. But emotionally, well, my fear is that I'll wake up one day and have no food and no money. I don't ever want to relive those times again. I guess that's why I find it so hard to spend my money today."

Her fear, which was so real when she was a child, was unreal in adulthood. But this fear influenced how she viewed money in the present and prevented her from feeling financially secure. My friend has since worked through her fears; today she lives comfortably, spends wisely, and is confident in her financial security for the future.

The key to achieving a strong sense of personal worth is to keep the value and meaning of money in perspective. You'll never be able to become financially secure as long as you woo money as you would a lover, chase after it with the determination of a hunter after the hunted, worship it as you would a god, hold onto past childhood fears about it, and pay more attention to it than you would yourself and those you love.

Think about this . . .

> "Money will buy a bed but not sleep; books but not brains; food but not appetite; finery but not beauty; a house but not a home; medicine but not health; luxuries but not culture; amusement but not happiness; religion but not salvation—a passport to everywhere but heaven."
>
> —Unknown

Making PERSONAL WEALTH LIFEGOALS can help you take control of your finances by identifying your assets and liabilities and by helping you examine where your money is going. Such knowledge can help you set financial goals and determine ways you can achieve those goals. Finally, PERSONAL WEALTH LIFEGOALS can assist you in initiating savings techniques that will increase your overall feeling of financial security.

PERSONAL WEALTH LIFEGOALS can help you work through such common conflicts as:

- *"Why can't I save more money from my earnings?"*
- *"How can I begin to live within my means?"*
- *"How can I alleviate some of my financial fears?"*
- *"In what ways can I increase my buying power?"*

When you make PERSONAL WEALTH LIFEGOALS, you're taking control of your financial future by actions and decisions you make now.

YOUR MISSION

To begin setting PERSONAL WEALTH LIFEGOALS, first determine the missions for your goals and outline them on the PERSONAL WEALTH MISSIONS CHART. Your missions are based on:

1. Your particular personal wealth problem areas (Who Are You Now?);

2. What you need or want from your goals (What Do You Want to Achieve?); and

3. The type of person you'd like to become or the life you'd like to have once you achieve your goals (Who Will You Be? or How Will You Be?).

PERSONAL WEALTH MISSIONS CHART

Who Are You Now?
Example: *I am a person who has a difficult time paying bills at the end of each month.*

1. _____

_____

2. _____

_____

What Do You Want to Achieve?
Example: *I need to have a little money left over at the end of every month, after I pay my bills, to begin a savings account.*

1. _____

_____

2. _____

_____

Who Will You Be? or How Will You Be?
Example: *I see a person who is able to effectively budget earnings and who can save money for future purchases.*

1. _____

_____

2. _____

_____

Your Mission
Example: *I want to create a goal that involves making a budget of my expenses and building in a savings plan, and to work with this budget for the next six months.*

1. _____

_____

2. _____

_____

YOUR FOCUS

Achieving Financial Security Through a Budget and Savings Plan

Your money-management skills are based on your *knowledge* of how much you bring in and how much you take out, your *ability* to manage this in-and-out cash flow so what you bring in is always greater than what you take out, and your *ability to save* from your earnings in order to build your financial security.

Your Knowledge: Examining Where Your Money Goes

To explore where the money you bring in goes, you might find it helpful to keep track of all your expenditures for three months. (You can then determine your average monthly expenses by dividing this amount by three.) Write down *everything* on which you spend your money, not just your major expenses. You'll be amazed at how much things like magazines, taxis, snacks, and so on, can deplete your earnings.

Then, based on the results of your tracking, figure out where you may be overspending each month. To do this, Dorlene V. Shane, a practicing certified fee-only financial planner, recommends that you compare the results of your monthly tracking to the following average national expenditures:

- **Housing:** rent, mortgage interest, utilities, furnishings, appliances.
  Allocate 30% of your monthly income.

- **Transportation:** gas, oil, car payments, repairs, commuting, tolls.
  Allocate 18% of your monthly income.

- **Food:** household purchases as well as restaurant meals.
  Allocate 18% of your monthly income.

- **Personal:** clothing, grooming, cosmetics.
  Allocate 12% of your monthly income.

- **Health Care:** doctors, hospitals, medications, eyeglasses, hearing aids.
  Allocate 9% of your monthly income.

- **Recreation:** hobbies, travel, sports, movies, videotape rentals.
  Allocate 4% of your monthly income.

- **Insurance:** automobile, home, health, life.
  Allocate 4% of your monthly income.

- **Miscellaneous:** donations, gifts, losses, installment and credit-card interest, property taxes.
  Allocate 3% of your monthly income.

- **Education:** tuition, books, publications, supplies.
  Allocate 2% of your monthly income.

To set PERSONAL WEALTH LIFEGOALS in the area of learning where your money goes, determine where you need to cut back on your spending and put into action ways to do this. For example, if you find that you're spending more than 4% of your monthly income on recreation, you might decide that you need to limit your nights out to once a week or once every two weeks. Or you might decide that you can best alleviate overspending of your current monthly salary by increasing the amount of money you have available to spend. In that case, you might want to ask for a raise or take on a part-time job.

The goal of developing your knowledge about where your money goes is to make you aware of how you use your money so you can determine the effectiveness of your spending.

Your Ability to Manage: Creating Your Budget

You may find it helpful to create your own personal budget as you track your expenditures for three months. Most office supply stores have budget books available, complete with heading entries. You might like to purchase one of these, or you may wish to create your own budget in a notebook or ledger book. Whatever method you choose for recording your income and expenses, be sure to create a budget that will work best for you and your lifestyle. *The goal of creating your own budget is to give you greater control over your money.*

When you set up your budget, it's important to account for *all* your expenses—from the morning newspaper to the bulb in the nightlight in your hallway—by noting these expenses *as they occur*. If you can't write them in right away, save your receipts so you can record them later.

What follows is a sample page from my own personal budget. Note that I enter my monthly income at the top of the page, then list the expenses below. At the end of every month, I add up the expenses, subtract them from my income, and record whether I have any money left over. This portion of your budget is integral in helping you determine the amount of "free money" you have left over for luxuries, donations, long-term goals, and a savings plan.

Month of JANUARY		
MONTHLY INCOME:		$1256.00
HOUSE EXPENSES		
Mortgage payment:	187.10	
*Property taxes:	58.30	
*House insurance:	29.16	
Appliances:	—	
Furnishings:	—	Total: 274.56
UTILITIES		
Electricity:	36.40	
Heat:	106.00	
Water/sewer:	29.60	
Telephone:	45.15	
T.V. Cable:	26.30	Total: 243.45
STAPLES		
Food:	240.00	
Personal hygiene:	40.00	Total: 280.00
TRANSPORTATION		
*Car insurance:	66.60	
Gas/oil:	40.00	
Repairs:	—	
Tolls:	—	
*Excise tax:	2.00	Total: 108.60
MEDICAL		
*Health insurance:	165.00	
Office visits:	—	
Prescriptions:	—	
Eye care:	—	Total: 165.00
LUXURY		
Clothing:	—	
Entertainment:	15.50	
Gifts:	—	
Miscellaneous:	—	Total: 15.50
TOTAL EXPENSES:		1087.11
INCOME LESS EXPENSES:		+ 168.89
MONEY LEFT OVER:		168.89

*These items are billed on a yearly basis, so I divide the total amount of the bill by 12 and set aside this portion each month.

Think about this . . .

> *The Japanese save 25% of their income; the average*
> *American saves only 5%.*
>
> —Dr. Edward Hallowell

Your Ability to Save: Becoming a Money-Saver

As you keep track of your expenditures for a few
months, you'll get an idea of the amount of "free money"
you have left at the end of each month. Ideally, you
should have *something* left, even if it's only a few dollars.
If you don't, you need to look at whether you're living beyond your means (taking out more money than you're
putting in) or spending a larger percentage of your earnings than you need to in certain areas.

If you aren't already in the habit of saving your
money, any savings plan you put into action will, at first,
require work. Your tendency will often be to spend the
"free money" or to find an immediate use for it. To get
around this, some savings experts recommend that you
enroll in an automatic savings program that takes money
out of your paycheck and puts it into a savings account.
Or you can increase your withholding by taking fewer
deductions than you deserve. In doing so, you set aside
more money than necessary to guarantee yourself a re-
fund when tax time rolls around.

These methods work well because usually, you won't
miss what you don't see!

However, if you have little "free money" left at the
end of each month, you may find that these savings op-

tions will take away money you don't feel comfortable setting aside. If you feel this way, you might try to cut down or set limits for expenditures in areas where you have some leeway—transportation costs (gas and oil), personal expenses (clothing, grooming, cosmetics), recreation (hobbies, travel, sports, movies, videotape rentals), the telephone bill, and so on, to free up extra cash.

If neither the automatic-style savings plans nor cutting down helps you to set aside money to place in a savings plan, you may find my "Loose Change" method helpful. Here's what I do: Rather than use my pocket change when making purchases, I save all my pennies, nickels, dimes, and quarters in a piggy bank. Each month, I roll my coins and deposit them in a savings account. Try it—you'll be amazed at how much money you set aside in this painless method!

The goal of becoming a money-saver is to be free of some of your financial worries and to gain greater financial independence by building up a resource of money aside from your income.

YOUR PERSONAL WEALTH LIFEGOALS

Now write your PERSONAL WEALTH LIFEGOALS. You may find the suggested Goal Starters helpful in creating your goals. Be sure your goals are specific to your personal wealth needs.

YOUR IMMEDIATE PERSONAL WEALTH GOAL(S): to be achieved with the next few minutes to the next few hours.

GOAL STARTER: *I want to open a savings account with five dollars.*

YOUR SHORT-TERM PERSONAL WEALTH GOAL(S): to be achieved within one week to one month.

GOAL STARTER: *I'm going to cut down on my weekly expenses each week for the next month.*

YOUR MID-TERM PERSONAL WEALTH GOAL(S): to be achieved within one month to one year.

GOAL STARTER: *For the next three months, I'm going to keep track of my expenditures.*

YOUR LONG-TERM PERSONAL WEALTH GOAL(S): to be achieved within two to four years.

GOAL STARTER: *I'd like to purchase a new car in two years, so I'll take $25 a week and put it into a savings plan.*

YOUR PERSONAL WEALTH TARGET GOAL(S): indefinite.

GOAL STARTER: *I'm going to meet with a financial advisor to determine the best ways to invest my money for the greatest returns.*

_____

_____

_____

READ ON

Creating Wealth, by Robert G. Allen, Simon & Schuster, 1986.

Finances After 50: Financial Planning for the Rest of Your Life, by Dorlene V. Shane, Harper & Row, 1989.

How to Invest $50–$5,000, by Nancy Dunnan, Harper & Row, 1987

New Money Book for the 80's, by Sylvia Porter, Avon Books, 1980.

Personal Finance and Home Management, by Robert Burns and Rees Johnson, Knight-Ridder Press, 1987.

Think & Grow Rich, by Napoleon Hill, Fawcett Crest, 1988.

Your Financial Security: Making Your Money Work at Every Stage of Your Life, by Sylvia Porter, Avon Books, 1989.

What Are You Worth? by Dr. Edward Hallowell, Weidenfeld and Nicholson, 1989.

8 □ LIFE CRISIS

How to Overcome Personal Crisis Through the Process of Healing and Recovery

 *A **life crisis** is an event or circumstance, or a reaction to an event or circumstance, that significantly interrupts or disturbs a person's healthy pattern of living **over a period of time** and/or causes a negative influence upon one or more areas of the individual's life.* Because the definition of life crisis contains many elements, further explanation of these elements is necessary.

Events or circumstances that can be considered examples of a life crisis include: the death of a loved one, personal injury or assault, termination of a love relationship, a chronic health problem or an illness, loss of a job, recognition of dysfunction in the childhood home, divorce, an addiction, etc.

Common reactions to such events or circumstances may be: a nervous breakdown, intense anger, emotional or mood swings, depression, lethargy, loss of sexual drive or interest, a desire to escape, overwhelming sadness, loss of appetite, sleeplessness (or, for some, the inability to get out of bed), anxiety, illness, personality changes, isolation, thoughts of suicide, increased used of drugs or alcohol, overeating, low self-image, and so on.

Keep in mind that most people experience these reactions, or similar ones, to events or circumstances that can be termed life crises. For example, it's perfectly normal for someone who has lost a parent to feel depression, overwhelming sadness, loss of appetite and intense anger, or for someone who has lost a job to have a low self-image and to feel anxious.

But when the event or circumstance, or the reaction to the event or circumstance, *significantly interrupts or disturbs a person's healthy pattern of living* **over a period of time** *and/or causes a negative influence upon one or more areas of the individual's life*, then particular attention needs to be paid to how that individual "gets through" the life crisis. The healthy "getting through" process, which involves healing and recovery, will be discussed in "The Focus" section of this chapter.

What happens when an event or circumstance interrupts or disturbs a person's healthy pattern of living over a period of time is that the person *changes the way he or she lives life, from the onset of the event or circumstance, and for a* **significant period of time** *thereafter.* Let me give you an example. In 1988, a friend's mother become ill and was diagnosed with cancer. Her mother died a year later. Shortly after, her father became ill with cancer. By the time the anniversary date of her mother's death rolled around, my friend's father required round-the-clock nursing care for his illness.

My friend's normal pattern of living was significantly interrupted and disturbed **over a period of time** by the life crises brought on by the back-to-back illnesses of her parents.

Although she was in college at the time, the flow of her life altered. No longer were classes, studying, working her part-time job, or socializing with friends part of her daily pattern of living. Instead, her life revolved around driving home, making hospital visits, and nibbling food brought over by neighbors and friends. The focus of her life became her mother's illness and death and her father's illness and impending death—not eating, sleeping, grades, friends, etc.

The key phrase to focus on in the definition of life crisis is *over a period of time*. Most of us experience setbacks, interruptions, or disruptions in the normal flow of our daily living. A car breaks down, you don't feel well, an important paper is lost, an accident happens, a conflict occurs. These aren't life crises—I consider them examples of hassles, problems, difficulties, or "things that have to be dealt with" that don't often take long to resolve—a day, a few days, a week, a few weeks, perhaps even a month.

But when an event or circumstance, or the reaction to an event or circumstance, is experienced for a period of at least *three months or more*, then I consider the event, circumstance, or reaction to the event or circumstance to be indicative of a life crisis. Disruption in a person's life that lasts for over a three-month period often dominates that individual's time to such an extent that "normal" or healthy patterns of living are usually suspended. This can have an incredible impact on the individual and on the way he or she lives life from that moment on.

Not all people react the same to similar life crises. The point of this chapter isn't to stress that anyone who goes through a life crisis needs to pursue some form of healing and recovery. *Some people grow on their own from life crises.* They become stronger individuals, more capable decision-makers, more appreciative of life and what it has to offer, and are better able to handle other life crises. Although their lives may be interrupted or disturbed for a significant period of time, they're often able to "bounce back" from tragedy or difficulties—sometimes with an even healthier attitude about themselves and about life. *Not everyone who undergoes a life crisis needs help.*

But some people don't grow, or don't know *how* to grow, from life crises. They stay stuck in their reactions to the event or circumstance and can't seem to get beyond the pain, sadness, shock, depression—whatever—caused by the life crises.

For example, my adoptive mother worshipped and adored her father. When he died when she was 26 years old, it's been said that she "never fully recovered" from his death for the rest of her life. She was an alcoholic, divorced once and twice a widow, who ended up dying unhappy and alone.

Think about this . . .

Roman statesman Marxus Aurelius has said, *"If you are distressed by anything external, the pain is not due to the thing itself, but to your estimate of it; and this you have the power to revoke at any moment."*

When a life crisis *causes a negative influence upon one or more areas of the individual's life over a period of time,* then some form of healing and recovery may be needed to help the individual work through the life crisis and grow from it. Negative influences from a life crisis can impact upon an individual's self-esteem, emotional development, maturity and personal growth, relationships, and the ability to communicate openly and honestly to others.

A person who grew up in a dysfunctional home, for instance, where the effects of such a life crisis are felt for years, usually leaves that home with established negative patterns of behavior. These patterns of behavior can prevent the individual from developing a strong sense of self-esteem, from forming healthy relationships, from knowing how to make healthy choices, etc.

Whether a life crisis is based in the past or occurs in the present, it's important to be aware of the methods of healing and recovery available should you or those you know need help in "getting through" the life crisis. These methods can be used as the basis for setting LIFEGOALS to help work through a life crisis and its residual effects.

Healing and recovery can help an individual resume a healthy pattern of living or can assist the person in changing negative behaviors brought about by the life crisis into positive ones. Healing and recovery can be facilitated by:

1. The Individual Alone

As I mentioned earlier, some people are capable of getting through (healing and recovering from) life crises on their own. However, unless the individual is already healthy, this type of "solo" work is rarely healthy. Those people who say, "I can handle it" or "I'm okay" and who take on the burden of their life crises alone—when they're not healthy nor have a strong emotional foundation on which to rely—often ignore the real issues raised by the effects of the life crises or deny that there's been any negative fallout from the life crises.

More often than not, people who effectively heal and recover "alone" usually do so as a result of the strong and supportive base of friends and family they know they can fall back on.

2. The Individual, with Material Support

Some people benefit from reading books and research materials on the subject of their life crises. I know many people who use Dr. Elizabeth Kubler-Ross' guidance and wisdom in *On Death and Dying* to help them through the loss of a loved one, for example. Other people can heal and recover by listening to motivational, inspirational, or meditation tapes; by journal writing; through prayer; etc. For me, reading *Adult Children of Alcoholics*, by Janet Woititz, helped begin my healing and recovery from a dysfunctional past by giving me the strength and courage to confront my mother's alcoholism and the effect it had upon my life.

3. By the Individual, With the Support of Family and Friends

One of my friends made it through months of criminal trials of three young men who had murdered her brother because her family love and support was strong.

Although the trials were difficult, she was able to let go of negative influences that could have impacted upon her because her family was always together at the trials and because they communicated openly and honestly with each other about their feelings.

On the other hand, a young man whose father was murdered found it difficult to handle the trials of the accused because his family base was dysfunctional and he was an isolator. So, he tried to "get through" his life crisis alone.

His inability to ask for help in healing and recovering from his tragedy perpetuated negative influences in his behaviors with others for a long period of time. He held on to intense anger for nearly two years afterwards, which ultimately destroyed his marriage and impacted upon his physical and emotional health. Until he used the next method to help in his healing and recovery, he found it difficult to cope each day.

4. By the Individual, With the Support of Others

Many find it helpful to work through life crises with the guidance of a therapist or counselor or with the support of self-help groups. These methods are often used by those who feel overwhelmed in major areas of their lives—relationships, work, personal emotions, and their direction or purpose in life—as a result of their life crises.

The most effective and long-lasting healing and recovery from a life crisis uses two or more of the four methods listed simultaneously. This discourages dependence on one method, encourages building relationships with family and friends, and promotes individual growth by developing the ability to gather answers from diverse sources and to make decisions and choices based on these answers.

Think about this . . .

"And remember, we all stumble, every one of us. That's why it's a comfort to go hand in hand."
—Emily Kimbrough

YOUR MOTIVATORS

Each of the following statements reflects some of the thoughts, feelings, and behaviors of a person who has been or is going through a life crisis. If you've experienced a life crisis or are yourself in the midst of a life crisis, you may find this list helpful in assessing the influence a life crisis has had or is having upon you. This list can also be useful in helping you help others who are experiencing life crises. You might like to share this list with them and ask them to think about how they feel about each of the following statements.

- *"I find it difficult to cope."*
- *"I wish I could go to sleep and not wake up."*
- *"I feel like I could explode."*
- *"I'd like to kill somebody."*
- *"I just want to scream."*
- *"Life's not fair."*

- *"I wish things would get better."*
- *"I wish everyone would leave me alone."*
- *"I'd like to go somewhere—anywhere!"*
- *"Sometimes I feel like I can't go on."*
- *"Everyone seems happy except me."*
- *"I feel alone."*
- *"I can't say how I feel."*
- *"I don't want to talk to anyone."*
- *"I feel drained."*
- *"I don't feel well."*
- *"I'm overwhelmed."*
- *"I can't stop crying."*
- *"Everything takes such effort."*
- *"I can't make up my mind about anything."*
- *"Nothing matters to me anymore."*
- *"Nobody cares."*
- *"I feel anxious."*
- *"I'm frightened."*
- *"It's all my fault."*
- *"Things will never get better."*
- *"I can't relax."*
- *"Nothing I do will make things better."*
- *"I'm a failure."*
- *"I'm no good."*
- *"I feel like I'm at the end of my rope."*

- *"I can't concentrate on anything."*
- *"It's the end of the world."*
- *"I'm unhappy."*
- *"I feel like I can't go on."*

If you experience any of these feelings during a life crisis, you may view life or your situation as hopeless. You may have little energy to do anything, even care for your basic needs—sleeping, eating, personal hygiene, etc. You may feel things will never "get better" or return to "normal." Time may seem to stand still, with the minute and hour hands on the clock locked into the moment when the life crisis began.

You may not know how to get on with your life, even when the climax of the life crisis has passed.

The purpose of setting LIFE CRISIS LIFEGOALS is to help you help yourself through the difficult time caused by the life crisis by working through the difficulty, not ignoring it; by focusing on the positive outcomes of the life crisis, even though you may only be able to see the negative; by learning how to use the guidance and support of others when it may be difficult for you to reach out for help; and by learning how to grow stronger as an individual from your experience, rather than lose strength and hope or feel defeated.

LIFE CRISIS LIFEGOALS can help you find answers to such questions as:

- *"What options are available to help me stop my addiction?"*
- *"Am I ready to confront my dysfunctional past?"*

- *"Can I let someone else reach out to me?"*
- *"Am I ready to trust another to guide me?"*
- *"Am I ready to admit that I can't do everything myself?"*

When you take responsibility for healing the wounds caused by a life crisis through actions that help you recover and grow in positive ways, then the rewards can be great. Instead of thinking or feeling any of the hopeless, negative statements listed earlier in this section, you can begin to experience hopeful, inspiring, and beneficial thoughts, feelings, and behaviors such as:

- *"I'm growing stronger every day."*
- *"I can let go of the past and look ahead to the future."*
- *"I believe things can get better."*
- *"It's not my fault; some things are out of my control."*
- *"I accept all my feelings."*
- *"I allow myself to express my feelings."*
- *"I can learn how to forgive."*
- *"I accept my self-defeating behaviors."*
- *"My healing and recovery are important and take priority."*
- *"I like when others reach out to me."*
- *"I feel safe and secure with myself."*
- *"I know I'm not alone."*
- *"Some happiness can come from sadness; some good can come from bad."*
- *"Each day is a new beginning."*
- *"I can get through today, a minute at a time."*

- *"Today is what matters, not yesterday nor tomorrow."*
- *"There's a reason for everything in this world."*
- *"I trust things will be okay."*
- *"Time heals all wounds."*
- *"I'm powerless over people, places, and things."*
- *"I believe in myself."*
- *"I'm responsible for my recovery, but I don't have to do it alone."*
- *"Sometimes asking the questions is more important than finding the answers."*
- *"I'm okay."*
- *"I'm getting better, a little bit at a time."*

YOUR MISSION

To begin setting LIFE CRISIS LIFEGOALS first determine the missions for your goals and outline them on the LIFE CRISIS LIFEGOALS CHART. Your missions are based on:

1. Your particular life crisis problem areas (Who Are You Now?);

2. What you need or want from your goals (What Do You Want to Achieve?); and

3. The type of person you'd like to become or the life you'd like to have once you achieve your goals (Who Will You Be? or How Will You Be?).

LIFE CRISIS MISSIONS CHART

Who Are You Now?
Example: *I am a person who probably has a drinking problem and needs to deal with it.*
1. _____

_____
2. _____

_____

What Do You Want to Achieve?
Example: *I want to stop drinking and work on improving my relationship with my family and friends.*
1. _____

_____
2. _____

_____

Who Will You Be? or How Will You Be?
Example: *I see a person who is healthy and happy and who has a wonderful family life, with a happy and healthy spouse and kids.*
1. _____

_____
2. _____

_____

Your Mission
Example: *I want to create a goal that will require me to attend A.A. meetings and to do marriage counseling.*
1. _____

_____
2. _____

_____

YOUR FOCUS

All About Healing and Recovery
From Life Crisis

You don't have to go through a life crisis in order to benefit from the information in this section, for it is designed to help you learn about two methods of healing and recovery—self-help groups and counseling—in case you or someone close to you is experiencing a life crisis and needs help.

Think about this . . .

American Indian philosopher Seneca has said, *"Remember that pain has this most excellent quality; if prolonged it cannot be severe, and if severe it cannot be prolonged."*

Simply stated, healing is like applying a "Band-aid" to the "wounds" caused by a life crisis. *Healing helps stop the "flow" of negative influences or reactions to a life crisis through a two-step process; first, identifying and acknowledging that there is a life crisis, and second, admitting that the life crisis or reaction to it has had or is having an effect on that person's life.*

Healing requires that the individual going through the crisis has an *awareness* about the crisis and its impact upon his or her life. Without this awareness, it will be difficult for someone to begin the process of healing.

For some, awareness comes from themselves, through

recognition of reactions to life crises such as negative or self-defeating actions, behaviors, or feelings. For example, when I recognized similar patterns of behavior and thinking in my intimate relationships—fear of abandonment, jealousy, irrational thinking, distrust, and so on—I realized I was acting out of reaction to the past abandonments I had experienced in my dysfunctional childhood. Once I had that awareness, I was ready to make changes (heal and recover) from those behaviors.

For others, awareness is acknowledged as a result of information provided by others, through discussion, confrontation or, in the case of some addictions, through the process of intervention (where individuals who play an important part in an addicted person's life confront the individual face-to-face and detail how the addiction has affected their relationship with him or her).

Sometimes those you know may not be aware of how a life crisis has affected them. It may be difficult for you to watch those you care for struggle or feel unhappiness when you know how much better the quality of their lives could be if only they were aware of their situation. *But personal growth comes from personal awareness*; sometimes the best you can do is to simply be there for them and show you care.

Recovery involves a three-part process, compiled into one whole—finding answers, using the answers to make changes, and growing over time. Recovery requires that the person going through the crisis *take action* to facilitate the healing process. *Taking action means setting goals that choose and use a combination of two or more of the four methods of healing and recovery mentioned earlier: relying upon oneself, using materials such as books and meditation, gathering sup-*

port from family and friends, and asking for help outside one's
circle of family and friends.

It's the latter method—asking for help outside one's
circle of family and friends—that people are often reticent
to use due to personal pride, not wanting to admit they
need help, or because they don't know what to expect.

Two resources that have proved to be extremely helpful to those experiencing a life crisis are *self-help groups*
and *therapy.* They are often viewed as effective methods
for facilitating recovery because of their ability to lead individuals using them to find answers on their own by
providing a dependable source of guidance, support, and
nurturing.

Self-Help Groups

The purpose of any self-help group is to offer support
for a particular area of sensitivity or focus for the group.
Alcoholics Anonymous was the forerunner of self-help
groups. Al-Anon formed next, followed in rapid succes-
sion by many other support groups: Narcotics Anonymous, Overeaters Anonymous, Gamblers Anonymous,
Emotions Anonymous, and numerous other "special interest" support groups for issues such as incest, cancer,
adoptees, bereavement, abused women, etc.

Self-help groups often follow a similar format. A person is selected to be the chairperson or speaker at the
meeting. This person may read or make an opening statement that briefly explains the purpose of the self-help
group and the format of the meeting. Then this person
may tell his or her "story" about how he or she was led

to the group. Often this story focuses on the past or present events and circumstances of this person's life and his or her actions, behaviors, or feelings. The story may last from five to twenty minutes.

The speaker may then talk about personal involvement in the self-help group and some of the benefits of recovery with the group.

The speaker will then open up the meeting to the rest of the group, encouraging them to share their thoughts and feelings about the speaker's story, about a topic of discussion chosen by the speaker, or about anything pertinent to the focus of the group. Sometimes members of the group will sit around a table or in chairs formed in a circle and speak, or choose to pass, in turn. Larger meetings may have chairs set up in rows; individuals choosing to speak can raise their hands and be recognized by the speaker.

Sharing by members is done for approximately an hour and a half. Some groups take a break in the middle of the meeting and have refreshments available; still others share without interruption for the entire time.

Not all self-help groups follow this format, but the general characteristics of a self-help group are: *a group facilitator* (who may be a group member, a professional such as a therapist, or someone who has an interest in or sensitivity to the focus of the group), a common purpose or focus (alcoholism, eating disorders, bereavement, etc.), and *a desire to share with and learn from others.*

For those in a life crisis, attending self-help group meetings can help them feel that they're not alone, that their feelings are similar to those of others who have had similar experiences, and that they can learn how to heal and recover by listening to others who are healing and recovering.

Attending meetings is an important step in recovery because the effects of a life crisis can be acknowledged—sometimes for the first time—in an atmosphere that's understanding, caring, and supportive.

Therapy

Talking with a licensed or trained social worker, therapist, counselor, or psychiatrist about the effects of a life crisis can have the same beneficial outcomes as a self-help group, but on a much deeper level.

Therapy is good for bringing out issues and developing new perspectives, both about yourself and about your life. It can also help you see yourself and the issues in your life with new clarity, often from a different perspective, so you learn more about yourself and how to deal with the events and circumstances in your life.

Therapeutic sessions usually run from 40 to 50 minutes in length. Some health insurance carriers offer limited coverage for psychotherapy; therapists often operate on a sliding scale fee for those who don't have coverage or for those whose coverage limit has been reached.

A good therapist helps the healing and recovery process by guiding the client towards finding personally appropriate solutions to individual difficulties. A good therapist doesn't tell the client what to do, but offers information based on research or experience. A good therapist encourages a human, open connection with the client and develops an atmosphere of trust, nurturing, gentleness, and support.

The goal of working with a therapist on life crisis issues or attending self-help group meetings is to be able to recognize five basic human rights and then to address these rights. When those who are experiencing life crises are ready to embrace these rights as their own, it can become easier for them to escape from the emotional upheaval of the life crisis and to begin the process of healing and recovery.

1. The Right to Be Free From the Past

You have a right to experience emotions in daily situations without feeling the effects of life crises from the past. You have a right to "close the files" on past thoughts, actions, and behaviors in order to fully experience living, loving, and learning in the present.

2. The Right to Learn a New Way of Life

You have a right to learn to live your life in a new way, by learning and growing from the experiences of your life crises.

3. The Right to Express Feelings

You have a right to have and to express your feelings regarding your life crises. You have a right to cry with others, to ask for hugs, to want encouragement and support, to show appropriate anger, and to verbalize pain.

4. The Right to Develop Self-Esteem.

You have the right to learn who you are, what you think, and how you feel so you can make decisions that are right for you.

5. The Right to Ask for Help.

You have the right to get advice, constructive criticism, hugs, support and companionship from others.

One final word about healing and recovery from a life crisis: There *is* a balance between "going it alone" and asking for help. *No one in this world is alone, unless they choose to be.*

YOUR LIFE CRISIS LIFEGOALS

Now write your LIFE CRISIS LIFEGOALS. You may find the suggested Goal Starters helpful in creating your goals. Be sure your goals are specific to your life crisis needs.

YOUR IMMEDIATE LIFE CRISIS GOAL(S): to be achieved within the next few minutes to the next few hours.
GOAL STARTER: *I'm going to call A.A.*

_____

_____

_____

YOUR SHORT-TERM LIFE CRISIS GOAL(S): to be achieved within one week to one month.

GOAL STARTER: *I'm going to talk to my best friend this week and share how I feel about my mother's death.*

_____

_____

_____

YOUR MID-TERM LIFE CRISIS GOAL(S): to be achieved within one month to one year.

GOAL STARTER: *I'm going to work with a career counselor to help me look for a new job. I'm also going to begin working with a holistic healer on ways I can reduce stress.*

_____

_____

_____

YOUR LONG-TERM LIFE CRISIS GOAL(S): to be achieved within two to four years.

GOAL STARTER: *I'm going to make a commitment to work with a therapist on my incest issues for at least two years.*

_____

_____

_____

YOUR LIFE CRISIS TARGET GOAL(S): indefinite.

GOAL STARTER: *I want to be able to deal with the pain of my search for my birth mother and the difficulties in our relationship. To achieve this, I'll read materials on other adoptees' searches, then start a self-help group in my area for adoptees and birth mothers.*

_____

_____

_____

RESOURCES

There are many books available today that focus on particular life crises and the process of healing and recovery from these crises. Your best bets, in pursuing further reading, are to explore the self-help sections of bookstores, to ask others who face or faced similar life crises what their recommendations are, or to consult your local library.

If you're interested in pursuing counseling as an option for healing and recovery, I highly recommend *How to Find a Good Psychotherapist: A Consumer Guide*, and *Can Psychotherapists Hurt You?* both by Judi Striano, Ph.D., Professional Press, 1987 and 1988, respectively.

The following list of resources can be used for more information about recovery options available for addictions or problems related to dysfunctional families. The addresses and telephone numbers listed are for the national headquarters; look in your local telephone book for resources closer to your area.

In addition to the following groups, other self-help organizations may be available in your area to assist your healing and recovery for particular life crises not listed here. For example, there may be groups designed to handle issues and provide support for: bereavement, cancer or chronic illness, widows and widowers, workaholism, rape, battered women, gays and lesbians, adoptees and birth mothers, etc. Consult your telephone directory, call a counseling center or help line near, or write or call:

National Self-Help Clearinghouse
33 West 42nd Street
New York, NY 10036
212-840-1259

Al-Anon Family Headquarters
(Al-Anon, for adults whose lives have been affected by the alcoholism of others; Alateen, for boys and girls, ages 11 to 18, whose lives are affected by the alcoholism of others)

1372 Broadway, 7th Floor
New York, NY 10018
800-245-4656

Alcoholics Anonymous (A.A.)
(for those whose lives are affected by drinking)

General Service Office
468 Park Avenue South
New York, NY 10016
212-686-1100

and

National Clearinghouse for Alcohol Information (NCALI)
P.O. Box 234
Rockville, MD 20852
301-468-2600

and
National Council on Alcoholism (NCA)
12 West 21st Street
New York, NY 10010
212-206-6770

and
**National Institute on Alcohol Abuse and
   Alcoholism (NIAAA)**
Parklawn Building, 5600 Fishers Lane
Rockville, MD 20852
301-468-2600

American Anorexia/Bulimia Association, Inc.
(for those suffering from eating disorders)

133 Cedar Lane
Teaneck, NJ 07666
201-836-1800

Children of Alcoholics Foundation
(for those from a dysfunctional childhood)

200 Park Avenue
31st Street
New York, NY 10166
212-949-1404

and
**National Association of Children of Alcoholics
   (NACOA)**
31706 Coast Highway
South Laguna, CA 92677
714-499-3889

Cocaine Anonymous
(for those affected by the use of cocaine)

National Office
P.O. Box 1367
Culver City, CA 90232
213-559-5833

and

National Cocaine-Abuse Hotline
800-COCAINE (262-2463)

Gamblers Anonymous
(for those whose lives are affected by gambling)

National Council on Compulsive Gambling
444 West 56th Street, Room 3207S
New York, NY 10019
212-765-3833

Incest Survivors Resource Network, International, Inc.
(for those who were sexually abused as children)

P.O. Box 911
Hicksville, NY 11802
516-935-3031

and

S.I.G.H. (Survivors of Incest Gaining Health)
20 West Adams, Suite 2015
Chicago, Illinois 60606

Narcotics Anonymous (NA)
(for those whose lives have been affected by drugs)

World Service Office
P.O. Box 9999
Van Nuys, CA 91409
818-780-3951

and

National Institute of Drug Abuse (NIDA)
Parklawn Building, 5600 Fishers Lane
Rockville, MD 20852
301-443-6245 (for information)
800-662-4357 (for help)

National Child Abuse Hotline
(for the treatment and prevention of child abuse)

Childhelp USA
P.O. Box 630
Hollywood, CA 90028
800-422-4453 (4-A-CHILD)

and

National Committee for Prevention of Child Abuse
332 South Michigan Avenue, Suite 950
Chicago, IL 60604
312-663-3520

Overeaters Anonymous
(for those suffering from eating disorders)

National Office
4025 Spencer Street, Suite 203
Torrance, CA 90504
213-542-8363

Parents Anonymous
(for parents under stress)

National Office
6733 South Sepulveda Boulevard, Suite 270
Los Angeles, CA 90045
800-421-0353

The National Rape Information Clearinghouse
(for those suffering from the trauma of rape)*

National Center for Prevention and Control of Rape
Park Lawn Building
5600 Fishers Lane
Rockville, MD 20857

and

National Coalition Against Sexual Assault
c/o Austin Rape Crisis Center
P.O. Box 7156
Austin, TX 78713
512-440-7273

---

*Also, contact your local rape crisis center in the event of an occurrence.

Students Against Suicide
(for teens affected by the suicide of other teens)

P.O. Box 115
South Laguna, CA 92677
714-496-4566

9 □ YOUR SPIRITUAL SELF

How You Connect Your Physical and Emotional Natures With A Spiritual Understanding

 Toward the end of Chapter Eight, I wrote, *"No one in this world is alone, unless they choose to be."* Building a relationship with your spiritual self ensures that you're never alone, even if you're the sole inhabitant of an island off the coast of Maine.

*Your **spiritual self** is created by your understanding of the connection between your physical nature (who you are), your emotional nature (how you feel), and the spiritual world (why you're here).*

When you connect your physical and emotional natures with some form of spiritual understanding, you may find that your life has more meaning. You may feel more "centered" in the universe, part of all that surrounds you. You may feel greater confidence in yourself, in who you are and what you do. And you may be more clear about your purpose and direction in life.

When you connect your physical and emotional natures with a spiritual understanding, you're creating a foundation of trust, faith, and belief in something bigger and more meaningful to your life than the people, places, and things in it. The world of your spiritual self combines what you know (the answers) with what you don't know (the questions).

*The ultimate goal of connecting your physical and emotional natures with a spiritual understanding is to **trust** your spiritual world—to feel safe and secure with both the answers **and** the questions.*

THE MOTIVATORS

Each of the following statements reflects some of the thoughts, feelings, and behaviors of a person who has developed or is developing a connection with his or her spiritual self. Do you relate to any of these statements?

- *"I know that a power greater than myself exists."*
- *"I trust that things in my life will work out."*
- *"I know my life has meaning."*
- *"I'm in tune with the universe."*
- *"I trust in the future."*
- *"I believe there's more good than evil in the world."*
- *"I appreciate the beauty of nature."*
- *"I respect the world I live in."*
- *"I do unto others as I'd like them to do unto me."*
- *"I listen to my intuitive side."*
- *"I believe in the power of prayer and meditation."*
- *"I know I'll find the answers I need, when I need them."*
- *"My life is full of joy."*

- *"Energy flows through me and out to the world."*
- *"I believe in making the world a better place for everyone."*
- *"I stay balanced despite the changes in my life."*
- *"I fill my life with positive, healing energy."*
- *"I experience peace and serenity in my life."*
- *"Each day is important to me."*
- *"Every day, I take time to notice and appreciate the people, places, and things around me."*
- *"There's no obstacle too great that it can't be overcome."*

People who are connected with their spiritual selves often see their glasses as half full, rather than half empty. Some think these people look at the world through rose-colored glasses because they usually manage to see the good in all people, places, and things. But their vision is often based on their faith and belief in the inherent good in everything and everybody.

These people are usually joyous and healthy individuals who are filled with energy and motivation to meet the challenges in their lives. They arise each day with a positive attitude and retire each night satisfied and secure with themselves and their place in the world.

When they suffer setbacks, experience losses, or feel pain or sadness, they're quick to trust that they will get through such difficulties. Their faith and belief in a power greater than themselves doesn't help them escape the bad times, but it helps pull them through such times. Often, they emerge from these experiences stronger and more secure with themselves and their world. As a result, they're often resilient to life's ups and downs and less likely to succumb to feelings of despair, hopelessness, or defeat.

People who are connected with their spiritual selves know that they aren't the center of the universe, that the world doesn't revolve around them or their needs. This knowledge often helps them develop a healthy perspective to set priorities and to determine what's most important in their lives.

People who are connected with their spiritual selves believe that finding the answers isn't as important as trusting that when the time is right, the answers will be revealed to them. Until then, they're content and secure in the knowledge that all is well with the world!

Why doesn't everyone have a connection with their spiritual selves?

I think part of the answer lies in an individual's background. Your knowledge of a spiritual connection is most often learned from your parents. If the focus in your childhood home was on an addiction or other dysfunction, then your family probably had little time or inclination to teach you how to develop a spiritual understanding. Your family life was most likely so wrapped up in the whirlwind of unhealthy behaviors in the home that you couldn't see beyond the four walls that surrounded you and the roof over your heads.

People who were brought up in dysfunctional childhood homes often have difficulty developing a spiritual understanding in adulthood. They learn to rely upon themselves. They often mistrust others and doubt the love that's shown to them. They may lack faith that things in their lives will get better. They can feel an overwhelming sense of hopelessness in the circumstances of their lives.

I grew up experiencing the pain, sadness, and daily uncertainties that are part and parcel of a dysfunctional home. A distinct memory I have about the role the spiritual world played in my life involved the feelings I had when I attended church with my parents every Sunday.

I hated going to church. There we were, sitting in a pew together, perceived by those who saw us as a loving family. I listened to the words of the minister. He talked about love, peace, harmony, trust, faith, and belief. He said, "God is always there. God will answer your prayers."

I remember bowing my head in prayer and asking God, "Why? Why do I feel so badly? When is this pain going to go away? When will I be happy? When will my parents show me love? When will we get along? What did I do that was so bad that You have to punish me now? Please, I'll do anything. Just make everything better."

Well, God didn't make everything better. Things stayed the same. I remained unhappy.

I lost hope that things would ever get better.

I tried to kill myself when I was 16. And again, when I was 23 and my life still wasn't better. By that time, however, I had already given up on God. I tried believing in myself, but I couldn't find much good in me.

For many years, I lived each day with very little faith, hope, or trust in the world around. It wasn't until I went through a life crisis and needed to confront my dysfunctional childhood that I realized that the spiritual world had never closed its doors to me; rather, I had shut myself off from receiving the peace, security, and love offered by a belief in something or someone outside of me.

Other reasons why people might not have a connection with the spiritual world in adulthood include: their determination to do things on their own, mistrust or doubt in the existence of a god-like being, dissatisfaction with structured religions, skepticism about New Age philosophies, and rejection of faith due to tragic life crises, to name a few.

But the reasons for a lack of spiritual understanding aren't as important as how this lack of spiritual understanding impacts upon the individual.

The impact is best described by the popular fable about the coat, the wind, and the sun.

Think about this . . .

One day the wind noticed a man, who was wearing a coat, walking down a path. The wind called out to the sun, "I'm more powerful than you, sun, and I can prove it. I bet I can make that man take off his coat."

The sun agreed to the bet and let the wind go first.

The wind blew fiercely upon the man, buffeting him with great gusts. The wind worked hard, but the man only gripped his coat even tighter around him.

"It's my turn," said the sun. The sun then shone brightly, sending rays of warmth to the man. The man paused, wiped his brow, then took off his coat. He draped the coat over his arm and continued on his way.

People who don't have a connection with the spiritual world often have a relationship with life like the interaction between the wind and the man. They keep their cloaks wrapped tightly around them, bow their heads, and proceed through life under their own power, determined to make it through each day as they struggle *against* the flow of life.

But people who are connected with the spiritual world have a relationship with life like that between the sun and the man. They shed their cloaks willingly and allow themselves to feel the warmth of the universe around them. They trust that they're safe and secure as they steadily move *along* the path of life.

You can develop a spiritual understanding by exploring the influence and impact four areas have upon your life and by including one or more of these areas in your daily living:

- *An appreciation of nature;*
- *A faith or belief in a higher power or power greater than yourself;*
- *A faith or belief in an overall life structure; and*
- *An intuition or sensitive perception of the world around you.*

Fostering a belief, faith, trust, or connection with one or more of these areas is what setting SPIRITUAL LIFEGOALS is all about.

YOUR MISSION

To begin setting SPIRITUAL LIFEGOALS, first determine a few missions for your goals and outline them on the SPIRITUAL MISSIONS CHART. Your missions are based on:

1. Your particular spiritual connection problem areas (Who Are You Now?);

2. What you need or want from your goals (What Do You Want to Achieve?); and

3. The type of person you'd like to become or the life you'd like to have once your achieve your goals (Who Will You Be? or How Will You Be?).

SPIRITUAL MISSIONS CHART

Who Are You Now?
Example: *I am a person who feels lost and hopeless from time to time.*
1. _____
_____
2. _____
_____

What Do You Want to Achieve?
Example: *I want to feel that I'm protected; that something or someone is watching over me.*
1. _____
_____
2. _____
_____

Who Will You Be? or How Will You Be?
Example: *I see a person who feels safe and secure, who trusts that things will turn out okay, and who is hopeful about the future, no matter what life brings.*
1. _____
_____
2. _____
_____

Your Mission
Example: *I want to create a goal that will encourage me to join a meditation group.*
1. _____
_____
2. _____
_____

YOUR FOCUS

Developing a Spiritual Understanding

The four areas I identified earlier can have a significant impact upon developing a spiritual understanding and connection in your life. The information that follows is designed to raise an awareness about each area.

This section is geared towards those who currently have little or no faith, trust, or belief in their lives; it's designed to help build a foundation for the creation of SPIRITUAL LIFEGOALS. But even if you already have some faith, belief, or trust in these or other spiritual connections, you may find the following information beneficial and even complementary to your own spiritual connection.

Think about this . . .

"There is a story of a religious teacher who used to talk every morning to his disciples. One morning he got on to the platform and was just about to begin when a little bird came and sat on the window sill. It began to sing, and sang away with a full heart. Then it stopped and flew away, and the teacher said, 'The sermon for this morning is over.' "

—J. Krishnamurti

Developing Your Spiritual Self Through An Appreciation of and Connection with Nature

Natural beauty can be spectacular. There's the bright, full moon, glowing orange or ethereal white, reflected on the shimmering waters of a lake, like silver streaks on a cool, black mirror. Or the vastness and color of the Grand Canyon, carved over eternities, a wonder of rushing waters and breathtaking vistas.

There's the power of the ocean, surging and crashing on shore, polishing stones and crushing shells, changing entire landscapes, yet, within its depths, embracing delicate coral and plant life with gentle undulations.

There's the change of seasons, a timeless wonder of hot, humid summers and crisp, colorful autumns; icicle-cold chilling winters and growing-green springs.

Many people have a spiritual connection with nature; they feel a certain sense of faith and trust in it. They marvel at its beauty and vastness, yet feel intimidated by its power. They're soothed by its rhythm—the change of seasons, the ebb and flow of the tide, the migration of birds, the rising and setting of the sun. While people have the ability to preserve or, unfortunately, to destroy, nature, they recognize that they do not have the power to create it. It's this creation, and the continuum of nature, that separates nature from humanity but also brings humanity closer to nature.

Sir Rabindranath Tagore once said, *"Faith is the bird that feels the light when the dawn is still dark."* The bird that sings long before the sun has risen is strong evidence of faith, for that bird trusts the sky will soon lighten, the sun will rise, and the world will come alive.

The day after a friend committed suicide, I awoke to a bright, sunny, early spring morning. The birds were singing and the smells of growth in the air were strong. I remember thinking, "She won't see what a glorious day it is today. Or what a wonderful spring this will be." I was saddened as much by her loss of faith that things wouldn't get better as by the loss of her. *It's when the bird won't sing that it has lost its faith in the great creation and continuum of all things natural.*

Appreciating nature and then "connecting" with it in some way—taking a walk in the woods or on the beach, camping, birdwatching, or whatever—can take you outside yourself and your small world, can help you forget (for a short time) your difficulties or problems, can open your mind and heart to new experiences, and can show you the wonder of something greater than you.

With an appreciation of nature, you can learn to believe that there isn't a problem that won't have a solution, a teardrop that won't have a smile, or a weary soul that won't be energized once again.

A goal to help you develop your spiritual self can include appreciating and connecting with nature, so you can realize a sense of faith, trust, and belief in its power to ensure that each day truly can be a new beginning.

Think about this . . .

"We cannot swing up a rope that is attached only to our own belt."

—William Ernest Hocking

Developing Your Spiritual Self Through Faith or Belief in a Higher Power or Power Greater Than Yourself

Many people feel that their ability to grow and change is directly related to how willing they are to admit they're not in control of everything in their lives, that there are some things which they're powerless to take control of on their own. This sense of powerlessness can be felt when working through a life crisis, making changes to live life in healthier ways, overcoming feelings of defeat or despair, or attempting to relieve feelings of loneliness.

You may feel that relying on yourself or on other people in your life doesn't always provide you with all the answers or help you need. Although you may be able to talk to a person or people in your life and derive some sense of comfort or understanding from these interactions, you may find these people can't necessarily give you everything you need to make your life better.

Where can you turn for help? Once you're ready to admit that you alone aren't capable of making everything better, you may be able to accept help from a spiritual source. That's what the phrase "a power greater than yourself" or the term "a higher power" means. Some people view this power as God, Buddha, Jehovah, etc.; as a sense of connection to the universe around them; or as a sense of faith and trust that they're taken care of.

You don't have to be "religious," believe in God, go to church, or read religious texts in order to believe in something greater than yourself. You just need to believe that you're not alone. Simply put, a belief in a power greater than yourself means you accept that you alone don't have all the power or control in your life, but that there *is* something or some being who can help you.

It means you can let go of the things you cannot change or figure out and can ask for help with these issues. Letting go doesn't mean releasing your grip on life and falling into an abyss below. Letting go is a gentle process of easing the grip you have on some facet of your life so you can open yourself up to change or enlightenment through the support of a power greater than you.

You can develop an understanding of a such a power through spiritual readings, through prayer and meditation, and by slowly learning to lose unnecessary control over people, places, and things in your life.

A goal to help you develop your spiritual self can be connecting with a power greater than yourself in some way so you can believe there's something or some being who can assist you in your life on a daily basis and/or when you feel you're powerless and need help.

Think about this . . .

"Sometimes I go about pitying myself and all the time I am being carried on great winds across the sky."
—American Indian saying

Developing Your Spiritual Self Through Faith or Belief in an Overall Life Structure

Most people, whether or not they identify themselves as spiritual, live their lives within the realms of a life structure. This structure is based on moral and/or ethical beliefs that they've been taught or have created for themselves. This life structure adds order to their lives and the world around them and provides guidelines for their growth and change.

The framework of most life structures is provided by the Golden Rule: *Do unto others as you would have them do unto you.* Treating others with courtesy, kindness, and respect; paying attention to the thoughts and needs of others; providing help to others when asked; and so on, are some of the ways you may choose to interact with people in your life—and want them to interact with you—because of your belief in the principle of the Golden Rule.

Other life structures are based on moral and ethical beliefs that govern an individual's perception of society and how the individual wants to behave within the social structure. Most people don't murder, rape, or steal. Most people don't willfully damage the property of others. Most people don't abuse animals or human beings—most people slow down when they see a squirrel crossing on the road ahead; they don't speed up.

Most people pay back loans. Most people aren't racist. Most people don't discriminate. Most people don't litter. Most people give to charities or those in need. Most people treat the environment with respect.

Belief in moral and ethical standards such as these can help you develop a connection between your physical and emotional natures and an overall "plan," or way of living. Even though laws govern most of society's moral and ethical standards, such laws are based upon centuries of human interactions and the struggle to create a structure that respects and preserves a high quality of life for everyone.

Besides living by the Golden Rule and by a set of moral and ethical standards, most people live by individual principles or rules they learned while growing up or which they created in adulthood: Respect your elders, hold the door for those behind you, be on time for appointments, do your best, and so on. These principles or rules, as well as the Golden Rule and moral and ethical structures, help bring order to your life, provide standards by which you choose to live, and determine the framework of your interactions with others. Living life by some structure creates a larger framework that addresses more than your day to day living—it gives purpose and meaning to your life.

A goal to help you develop your spiritual self can be creating and living a life structure that supports beliefs that are right for you, where you can change these beliefs when necessary, but don't compromise them for personal gain or because others want you to.

Think about this..

"Prayer is when you talk to God; meditation is when you listen to God."
—quoted by Diana Robinson
in *The People's Almanac*

Developing Your Spiritual Self Through Intuition or Sensitive Perception of the World Around You

In developing an intuition or sensitive perception of the world around you, you're like a radio receiver that picks up the signals beamed to it from all directions. Some of these signals are from people, some are from yourself, some are from the world around you, some are from a power greater than yourself.

Most people tend to "tune in" to their own signals or the signals sent to them by others through conversation. They tend to "tune out" gut instincts ("I feel that I mustn't board this airplane; it's going to crash."), feelings ("I don't trust what he's telling me."), unexplained thoughts ("Maybe you ought to call your daughter to make sure she made it home okay."), "voices" (such as those which Joan of Arc said she heard), and so on. They may dismiss these "tuned out" messages as poppycock or term them irrational, preferring to believe what they can see, hear, taste, touch, and smell rather than having faith in something they merely sense.

One of my friends has a good instinct for people. She can usually "feel" what a person is like and determine right away whether that person can be trusted, is honest, is dependable, is stable, and so on. My friend is almost always right about her perceptions. While she can't explain her ability to intuitively "know," she simply trusts that, for whatever reasons, the messages she receives have meaning and purpose in her life.

A goal to help you develop your spiritual self includes "tuning in" to your intuition or sensitive perception of the world and "listening" to the signals you receive by "opening" up all your channels. You can do this through meditation, by allowing yourself to trust more of your instincts, and by becoming more aware of your feelings (see Chapter Two).

In the beginning of this chapter, I mentioned the impact that the lack of spiritual beliefs had earlier in my life. While I was once suicidal, today I have faith, trust, and belief in a power greater than myself. I've developed a connection with nature. I live my life with a moral and ethical structure and try to treat others as I'd like them to treat me. Through meditation, I'm able to be more receptive to the world around me.

I could only do this through healing and recovery from my dysfunctional childhood. There were people in Al-Anon and Adult Children of Alchoholics groups who helped me see that I wasn't the most important person in the world and that my childhood circumstances weren't unique. There were great books I read from authors who encouraged me to open my eyes to the world around me. There were therapists who guided me gently through the pain and loss in my life and helped me trust that my life could be different. And there was a simple gift—a bird watcher's book—with the inscription "Here is where trust begins," that led me to the beauty and inspiration of nature.

Your spiritual world develops slowly, through patience, understanding, hope, and trust. Keep this in mind as you set your SPIRITUAL LIFEGOALS. Try not to focus on outcomes as much as the small changes that can happen within yourself.

YOUR SPIRITUAL LIFEGOALS

Now write your SPIRITUAL LIFEGOALS. You may find the suggested Goal Starters helpful in creating your goals. Be sure your goals are specific to your spiritual needs.

YOUR IMMEDIATE SPIRITUAL GOAL(S): to be achieved within the next few minutes to the next few hours.
GOAL STARTER: *I'm going to purchase a meditation book.*

YOUR SHORT-TERM SPIRITUAL GOAL(S): to be achieved within one week to one month.
GOAL STARTER: *I'm going to take a long walk by myself on the beach, every two weeks.*

YOUR MID-TERM SPIRITUAL GOAL(S): to be achieved within one month to one year.
GOAL STARTER: *I'm ready to let go of trying to solve all my problems myself. I want to start developing a connection with a higher power by praying each night.*

YOUR LONG-TERM SPIRITUAL GOAL(S): to be achieved within two to four years.

GOAL STARTER: *I want to attend a variety of spiritually-oriented workshops over the next few years to explore different experiences to combine with a career in holistic healing.*

YOUR SPIRITUAL TARGET GOAL(S): indefinite.

GOAL STARTER: *It's important for me to live closer to nature. To that end, I'm going to start a weekly savings plan so I can eventually buy or build a cabin in the woods of Vermont.*

READ ON

There are many books, videos, and tapes available today to help individuals connect their physical and emotional natures with a spiritual understanding. The following listed materials are books I've found helpful in developing my own spiritual connection. You may wish to browse in self-help sections of bookstores or in New Age bookshops before you make your own selections. Refer also to the "Read On" section of Chapter Three for a listing of suggested meditation tapes.

A World Beyond, by Ruth Montgomery, Fawcett Crest, 1971.

Came to believe . . . , by Alcoholics Anonymous World Services, Inc., 1973 (many reprintings).

Gift from the Sea, by Anne Morrow Lindbergh, Vintage Books, 1955 (many reprintings).

The House by the Sea, A Journal, by May Sarton, W. W. Norton & Company, 1977.

Living, Loving & Learning, by Leo Buscaglia, Ph.D., Fawcett Columbine, 1982.

Living on the Earth, by Alicia Bay Laurel, Vintage Books, 1971.

*Meditation Gift Set for Women/Meditation Gift Set for Men, Hazelden Publishers; contains five different meditation/inspirational books.

The Outermost House, by Henry Beston, Penguin Books, 1928 (many reprintings).

Out on a Limb, by Shirley MacLaine, Bantam Books, 1983.

The Prophet, by Kahlil Gibran, Alfred A. Knopf (many reprintings).

The Road Less Traveled, by M. Scott Peck, M.D., Simon and Schuster, 1978.

Woman Spirit: A Guide to Women's Wisdom, by Hallie Iglehart, Harper & Row, 1983.

Working Inside Out, by Margo Adair, Wingbow Press, 1984.

*Can be ordered from Hazelden Educational Materials by calling 1-800-328-9000.

How to Continue Growing
Through LIFEGOALS

 If I could leave you with one recommendation to help you keep your LIFEGOALS work in perspective, it would be: *Don't let reaching your goals deprive you of making interesting detours.* It's okay to set goals and to do all that's possible to attain them, but don't do so at the expense of missing out on wonderful, fun, exciting, or challenging non-goal-oriented adventures. It's great to have a destination, but it's even better to reach that destination after making some terrific side trips.

If I could leave you with one guideline to help you make goal-setting decisions that are right for you, it would be: *Be yourself.* Don't set goals you hope will make you into someone you aren't. I once saw a cartoon that showed a couple arriving at a party. As they were greeted at the door, they announced, "Sorry we're late, but that's our style." Don't expect your goals to make radical changes in you. Let your goals be true to you and your lifestyle.

If I could leave you with one tool to help you set LIFEGOALS now and in the future, it would be: *Evaluate the results of every goal you set.* If you don't achieve your goals, find out why. If you do achieve your goals but aren't happy with the results, think about what would make you happy. If you do achieve your goals and are happy with the results, then set new goals.

Successful setting of LIFEGOALS is the continual process of making a goal and achieving it, making another goal and achieving it, making still more goals and achieving them.

To help you evaluate the goal setting you've done so far or may do in the future in each of the seven areas discussed in this book, you may wish to fill out the following charts or think about your responses to the questions posed.

SELF-ESTEEM LIFEGOALS

YOUR IMMEDIATE GOAL(S)
Did you achieve your goal(s)? _____
If not, why? _____

_____
Your new goal(s): _____

_____

YOUR SHORT-TERM GOAL(S)
Did you achieve your goal(s)? _____
If not, why? _____

_____
Your new goal(s): _____

_____

YOUR MID-TERM GOAL(S)
Did you achieve your goal(s)? _____
If not, why? _____

_____
Your new goal(s): _____

_____

YOUR LONG-TERM GOAL(S)
Did you achieve your goal(s)? _____
If not, why? _____

_____
Your new goal(s): _____

_____

YOUR TARGET GOAL(S)
Steps used to work towards your goal(s):

_____
_____
_____

HEALTH AND FITNESS LIFEGOALS

YOUR IMMEDIATE GOAL(S)
Did you achieve your goal(s)? _____
If not, why? _____
_____

Your new goal(s): _____
_____

YOUR SHORT-TERM GOAL(S)
Did you achieve your goal(s)? _____
If not, why? _____
_____

Your new goal(s): _____
_____

YOUR MID-TERM GOAL(S)
Did you achieve your goal(s)? _____
If not, why? _____
_____

Your new goal(s): _____
_____

YOUR LONG-TERM GOAL(S)
Did you achieve your goal(s)? _____
If not, why? _____
_____

Your new goal(s): _____
_____

YOUR TARGET GOAL(S)
Steps used to work towards your goal(s):
_____
_____
_____

RELATIONSHIP LIFEGOALS

YOUR IMMEDIATE GOAL(S)
Did you achieve your goal(s)? _____
If not, why? _____
_____

Your new goal(s): _____
_____

YOUR SHORT-TERM GOAL(S)
Did you achieve your goal(s)? _____
If not, why? _____
_____

Your new goal(s): _____
_____

YOUR MID-TERM GOAL(S)
Did you achieve your goal(s)? _____
If not, why? _____
_____

Your new goal(s): _____
_____

YOUR LONG-TERM GOAL(S)
Did you achieve your goal(s)? _____
If not, why? _____
_____

Your new goal(s): _____
_____

YOUR TARGET GOAL(S)
Steps used to work towards your goal(s):
_____
_____
_____

COMMUNICATION LIFEGOALS

YOUR IMMEDIATE GOAL(S)
Did you achieve your goal(s)? _____
If not, why? _____
_____
Your new goal(s): _____
_____

YOUR SHORT-TERM GOAL(S)
Did you achieve your goal(s)? _____
If not, why? _____
_____
Your new goal(s): _____
_____

YOUR MID-TERM GOAL(S)
Did you achieve your goal(s)? _____
If not, why? _____
_____
Your new goal(s): _____
_____

YOUR LONG-TERM GOAL(S)
Did you achieve your goal(s)? _____
If not, why? _____
_____
Your new goal(s): _____
_____

YOUR TARGET GOAL(S)
Steps used to work towards your goal(s):
_____
_____
_____

CAREER/LIFEWORK LIFEGOALS

YOUR IMMEDIATE GOAL(S)
Did you achieve your goal(s)? _____
If not, why? _____
_____
Your new goal(s): _____
_____

YOUR SHORT-TERM GOAL(S)
Did you achieve your goal(s)? _____
If not, why? _____
_____
Your new goal(s): _____
_____

YOUR MID-TERM GOAL(S)
Did you achieve your goal(s)? _____
If not, why? _____
_____
Your new goal(s): _____
_____

YOUR LONG-TERM GOAL(S)
Did you achieve your goal(s)? _____
If not, why? _____
_____
Your new goal(s): _____
_____

YOUR TARGET GOAL(S)
Steps used to work towards your goal(s):
_____
_____
_____

PERSONAL WEALTH LIFEGOALS

YOUR IMMEDIATE GOAL(S)
Did you achieve your goal(s)? _____
If not, why? _____

_____

Your new goal(s): _____

_____

YOUR SHORT-TERM GOAL(S)
Did you achieve your goal(s)? _____
If not, why? _____

_____

Your new goal(s): _____

_____

YOUR MID-TERM GOAL(S)
Did you achieve your goal(s)? _____
If not, why? _____

_____

Your new goal(s): _____

_____

YOUR LONG-TERM GOAL(S)
Did you achieve your goal(s)? _____
If not, why? _____

_____

Your new goal(s): _____

_____

YOUR TARGET GOAL(S)
Steps used to work towards your goal(s):

_____

_____

_____

LIFE CRISIS LIFEGOALS

YOUR IMMEDIATE GOAL(S)
Did you achieve your goal(s)? _____
If not, why? _____
_____

Your new goal(s): _____
_____

YOUR SHORT-TERM GOAL(S)
Did you achieve your goal(s)? _____
If not, why? _____
_____

Your new goal(s): _____
_____

YOUR MID-TERM GOAL(S)
Did you achieve your goal(s)? _____
If not, why? _____
_____

Your new goal(s): _____
_____

YOUR LONG-TERM GOAL(S)
Did you achieve your goal(s)? _____
If not, why? _____
_____

Your new goal(s): _____
_____

YOUR TARGET GOAL(S)
Steps used to work towards your goal(s):
_____
_____
_____

SPIRITUAL LIFEGOALS

YOUR IMMEDIATE GOAL(S)
Did you achieve your goal(s)?_____
If not, why?_____
_____

Your new goal(s): _____
_____

YOUR SHORT-TERM GOAL(S)
Did you achieve your goal(s)?_____
If not, why?_____
_____

Your new goal(s): _____
_____

YOUR MID-TERM GOAL(S)
Did you achieve your goal(s)?_____
If not, why?_____
_____

Your new goal(s): _____
_____

YOUR LONG-TERM GOAL(S)
Did you achieve your goal(s)?_____
If not, why?_____
_____

Your new goal(s): _____
_____

YOUR TARGET GOAL(S)
Steps used to work towards your goal(s):
_____
_____
_____

Finally, if I could leave you with one inspirational thought that could motivate you to continue making LIFEGOALS in each of the seven areas for the rest of your life, it would be this:

Think about this . . .

> *"It must be borne in mind that the tragedy of life doesn't lie in not reaching your goal. The tragedy lies in having no goal to reach. It isn't a calamity to die with dreams unfilled, but it is a calamity not to dream. It is not a disgrace not to reach the stars, but it is a disgrace to have no stars to reach for."*
>
> —emeritus college president
> Benjamin E. Mays

Without goals, it's easy to lose yourself. Without goals, it's difficult to know which direction to head in. Without goals, it's hard to find a purpose and meaning in life.

Goals are the stars by which you navigate your ship of life; it's up to you to create these stars, to light these stars, to place them in clear view, and to move towards them.

ABOUT THE AUTHOR

Amy E. Dean is the author of bestselling books on the subject of Adult Children From Dysfunctional Familes, published by Hazelden Educational Materials: *Night Light, Once Upon a Time: Stories From Adult Children,* and *Making Changes: How Adult Children Can Have Healthier, Happier Relationships.*

She is a frequent lecturer on the subject of healing and recovery from a dysfunctional past. Her message is based on the strength and hope of her own recovery from a background of dysfunction. She has also designed and implemented a course in recovery for Adult Children, called "Growing Up Again." Goal-setting and goal-achieving are the focus of this course.

Ms. Dean lives in Maynard, Massachusetts.

If you would like to receive a catalog of Hay House products, or information about future workshops, lectures, and events sponsored by the Louise L. Hay Educational Institute, please detach and mail this questionnaire.

We hope you receive value from *Lifegoals*. Please help us evaluate our distribution program by filling out this brief questionnaire. Upon receipt of this postcard, your catalog will be sent promptly.

NAME _____

ADDRESS _____

_____

I purchased this book from:

☐ Store _____

City _____

☐ Other (Catalog, Lecture, Workshop)

Specify _____

Occupation _____ Age _____

We hope you receive value from *Lifegoals*. Please help us evaluate our distribution program by filling out this brief questionnaire. Upon receipt of this postcard, your catalog will be sent promptly.

NAME _____

ADDRESS _____

_____

I purchased this book from:

☐ Store _____

City _____

☐ Other (Catalog, Lecture, Workshop)

Specify _____

Occupation _____ Age _____

Place
Stamp
Here

To: HAY HOUSE, INC.
P.O. Box 2212
Santa Monica, CA 90407

Place
Stamp
Here

To: HAY HOUSE, INC.
P.O. Box 2212
Santa Monica, CA 90407